Middle Ages

Stories, Activities, and Reproducibles to Connect Reading and Writing with Social Studies

Tara McCarthy

SCHOLASTIC

ISBN 0-590-25103-1

The Middle Ages

by Tara McCarthy

SCHOLASTIC
PROFESSIONAL BOOKS

New York · Toronto · London · Auckland · Sydney

For Alison and Beryl

Designed by Sydney Wright
Cover design by Vincent Ceci and Frank Maiocco
Cover photo © Giraudon/Art Resources, New York.
Loire Valley atelier, 16th century. Tapestry of the Seignorial Life: the Lesson. Paris, France, Musee de Cluny.
Interior illustration by Jim McConnell
ISBN: 0-590-25103-1
Copyright © 1995 by Tara McCarthy. All rights reserved.
12 11 10 9 8 7 6 5 4 3 2   4 5/9
Printed in the U.S.A.

Table of Contents

Introduction   4

1. Beowulf
Teacher Pages   8
Reproducible: A Picture Chart   13
Story   14

2. How Arthur Became King
Teacher Pages   22
Story   28

3. The Dapple-Gray Palfrey
Teacher Pages   35
Reproducible: Manuscript Border Designs   40
Story   41

4. The Story of the Little Bird
Teacher Pages   48
Reproducible: A Story Chart   53
Story   54

5. The Three Thieves
Teacher Pages   58
Story   63

6. Robin Hood and the Widow's Sons
Teacher Pages   69
Story   75

7. The Canterbury Tales
Teacher Pages   79
Reproducible: A Knowledge Chart   87
Story: *An Introduction to The Canterbury Pilgrims*   88
Story: *The Wife of Bath's Tale*   91
Story: *The Pardoner's Tale*   96
Story: *The Nun's Priest's Tale*   100

Glossary   104

Annotated Bibliography for Teachers   105

Annotated Bibliography for Students   107

Introduction

Knights and castles; cathedrals and stained-glass windows; troubadours and tournaments; lords, ladies, and serfs; crusades and craft fairs—most students in the middle grades love to read about the Middle Ages and may already know a lot of facts about this turbulent, boisterous, exciting period of history. Indeed, by drawing on students' prior knowledge and enthusiasm, many teachers build theme units around the medieval period.

Fortunately, there are many factual accounts of the era, designed for classroom use. But what is the "glue" teachers can use to bring all these facts together? How do we provide students with a sense of *why* people of that time thought and acted as they did? How can students get a sense of the ambiance of the Middle Ages, of the social, cultural, and political forces that affected behavior and motivated change? Literature provides the key.

STORIES AS MIRRORS OF AN AGE

The ten stories in this book are not *about* the Middle Ages. Rather, they are adaptations of stories people *told* in the Middle Ages. Whether myth, legend, fantasy, or fable, the stories reflect—as all traditional literature does—the beliefs and concerns of the storytellers and the audience and provide a glimpse of the way people of those days lived.

When referring to Western Europe, the term *Middle Ages* means that vast sweep of time from approximately A.D. 500 to the mid-1400s. This time is also known as the medieval period. In this span of 1,000 years, people's beliefs and concerns, as well as their lifestyles, evolved and changed radically. The stories here—from *Beowulf* to *The Canterbury Tales*—are presented in an order roughly representing the sequence of their origin. Thus, as students enjoy the stories sequentially, they travel through medieval times from the rough-and-tumble days of the Germanic invasions, through the establishment of feudalism and the manorial system, to the decline of medieval times and the rise of the Renaissance.

TEACHING FOR DEPTH

The popular stories of any era occur in a social context: momentous historical events, customs, political upheavals, and economic patterns. Stories both reflect this context and also show people's reaction to it. The teaching sections that preface each story are designed to help you stress both the literary aspects of the tale and the social setting in which the story developed. Follow-up activities and further-reading suggestions provide ways for students to broaden both their appreciation of medieval literature and their understanding of the context in which the story was told. In turn, as students move on to the next tale they can compare its literary elements with previous ones and also see how it reflects changing times.

USING THE POSTER

Build enthusiasm for the stories by displaying the A Walk Through the Middle Ages poster right away. By referring to the people, buildings, and places

shown in the poster, students can preview stories and get ideas for stories and research reports of their own. Just as important, the poster provides a stunning visual summary of major concepts about the Middle Ages and a way for students to trace and retrace the social history of that era. The Teaching Sections include suggestions for using the poster with individual stories.

HOW THE TEACHING SECTIONS ARE ORGANIZED

1. The **Story Summary** provides you with an overview of the tale and some literary background about it, which you may wish to share with students.

2. In **Building Social Studies Background**, you'll find suggestions for ways to preview the story through drawing on students' prior knowledge and through strategies such as map study, discussion and prediction questions, and developing links between our world and the world of the Middle Ages. In several cases, the **Background** also supplies you with extended comments that will help you add to and enrich the students' discussions.

3. Each story can be approached through a different **Suggested Reading Strategy**. Some strategies, such as glossing and tableaux, actually originated during the Middle Ages. Other strategies include reading aloud, making story charts, asking questions, and directed reading.

4. By using the suggestions in **After Reading**, students link what they've read to the major activity they'll undertake.

5. Next comes a description of the major **Student Activity** and steps for implementing it. These activities encourage students to deepen their understanding of the stories and to expand upon them by using them as models for their own creative work.

6. **Additional Activities** provide further ideas for developing the social studies aspects of the stories, as well as suggestions for expanding and enriching other areas of the curriculum with students' growing understanding of life in Middle Ages.

OTHER USEFUL FEATURES

♦ Four reproducible **Activity Sheets**

♦ A **Glossary** (page 104) with definitions of literary and historical terms from the Middle Ages

♦ An **Annotated Bibliography for Teachers** (pages 105-106) to help you investigate further certain aspects of this fascinating period in history

♦ An **Annotated Bibliography for Students** (pages 107-112) to help you choose books and other follow-up resources for your students

Beowulf

Story Summary

The vassals of King Hrothgar (rōt´ gär) of Denmark fall victim to Grendel, a monster who lives beneath the water. Beowulf (bā´ō wülf), a young noble from Jutland, comes to Hrothgar's aid and after many trials and battles succeeds in killing Grendel and Grendel's monster mother. In this condensed prose retelling of the epic, students can detect how early medieval rulers gained power and the loyalty of their vassals, or knights, and how each knight played various roles.

Beowulf is usually considered the first great work of English literature. Like all epics, *Beowulf* is an extended narrative poem that recounts the triumphs and tragedies of a hero. Its 3,200 lines of alliterative verse were written down in Old English (Anglo-Saxon) by an unknown poet c. A.D. 700. The story itself is much older: It has its origins in Norse myth blended with historical events in Denmark. Danish invaders carried the story to England, where it was fused with Christianity, became immensely popular among people in all walks of life, and—told and retold orally through the centuries—took on details that vividly reflect the feudal system that existed in England and France.

Building Social Studies Background

1. Preview—Using the Poster: Students can compare the description of an early castle on page 15 with the castle shown in the poster. Direct their attention especially to the fortlike, defensive features of the poster castle (high wall, turrets, etc.).

2. The Setting of the Story. On a map of Northern Europe, have students locate Denmark. Explain that an island off the coast was the ancient site of the castle of the King of the Danes. Then point out the coast of southern Sweden (Jutland, in the story) facing the Danes and explain that this area was once the home of the Geats, the tribe of people to which Beowulf belonged.

Since much of the story takes place under or near the water, students might discuss what they know about northern seas and the life-forms in them (seals, whales, etc.)

3. Real Heroes and Superheroes. Explain that the hero of this story performs many fantastic deeds, but that the character of Beowulf, superhuman though he has become in myth, is probably based on a real historical character, an ordinary human who in his lifetime performed believable acts of courage. If your students are familiar with the stories of historical heroes like Paul Revere, Daniel Boone, and Calamity Jane, you might ask them to recall what these people were like in real life and what fantastic embroideries were added to their stories through the years. You may wish to share with students the background information about the story of Beowulf. (See Story Summary.)

A SUGGESTED READING STRATEGY

Glossing. The practice of *glossing*, or writing marginal notes, arose during the Middle Ages and continues to be a good strategy for commenting on or asking questions about a literary text. A good way for your students to gloss *Beowulf* is to provide each student with a copy of the story, then have students work with a partner or small group to read the story together and write their questions and ideas in the margin in pencil. However, if you don't want students to write on the story pages, have them write their notes on notebook paper aligned with the text pages.

Outline strategies for glossing *Beowulf*, for example:

♦ **Read with a Purpose:** Find out about the relationship between lords and their knights. What did the lord or king owe to the knights? What did they owe to him?

♦ **Use Prior Knowledge:** What other stories come to your mind as you read about Beowulf?

♦ **Organize New information:** How is Beowulf like a real-life hero? How is he like a fantasy hero?

♦ **Draw Conclusions:** Why do you think people of the Middle Ages liked this story?

Also encourage students to note words and phrases they would like to define and to ask questions about parts of the story they would like to discuss.

Provide a model on the chalkboard or overhead projector of how one paragraph might be glossed. Example:

Soon Hrothgar himself had gained immense wealth through his constant warfare. He decided to use much of his wealth to build a huge hall, or stronghold, which he would name Heorot. "At Heorot," he said, "I shall entertain my knights with feasts and music. In my great hall, we shall listen to the troubadours as they sing us stories of heroes. Best of all, Heorot will be strong enough to protect us from our enemies."

I guess the kings spent all their time fighting. What's a stronghold? maybe its like a fort.

For months and months, workers labored with shovels, hammers, and chisels to build Hrothgar's hall, mound by mound. On the day when Heorot was completed, the gate was thrown open, and the knights and all the court entered the magnificent room. They were awed by its size and delighted with the feast Hrothgar had readied for them. What a pleasure it was, too, to hear the troubadour's songs, for many of them told about Hrothgar himself and his brave company of knights.

I want to find out about the building materials.

A castle with just one room?

After Reading Ask partners to share and discuss with the class the glosses they've made. Encourage students to help one another explain passages in the story and to use a dictionary to clarify any words and phrases they've highlighted. Discuss how glossing helps readers not only to read closely but also to raise important questions about the text. Some students may have ideas about how glossing can help them do close studies of other texts, both fiction and nonfiction.

STUDENT ACTIVITY
♦♦♦ Developing A Picture Chart of Feudal Roles ♦♦♦

Before handing out copies of the the Many Roles of a Knight reproducible on page 13, help students firm up their understanding of (1) the basic feudal relationship between lords (kings) and vassals (knights, or barons), and (2) warfare as the major activity of a lord and his vassals. To help students visualize these concepts, copy the following chart on the chalkboard. Discuss the questions with students and have them write their conclusions in the arrows. (Here, probable answers are given in parentheses.)

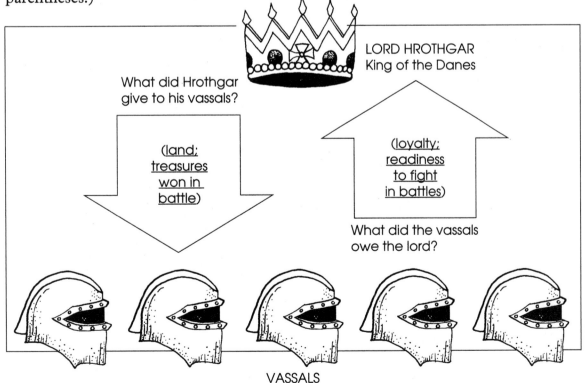

Next, hand out the Many Roles of a Knight reproducible (page 13) and suggest that partners discuss and answer the questions together, based on their reading of *Beowulf*. (Probable responses: 1. He was the nephew of the King of the Geats; 2. the King of the Geats; the King of the Danes; 3. He killed monsters. He fought by his uncle's side in wars; 4. the 14 knights who accompany him to Denmark). In response to the question below the chart, partners can write their ideas and then share them with a larger group.

ADDITIONAL ACTIVITIES

✦✦✦ Art ✦✦✦

Beowulf in Pictures *Beowulf*, because of its superhero aspects, invites a retelling through comic book–style picture panels with captions and dialogue balloons. A small group of students may wish to work on this project together. Ask the group to decide first on the major incidents and ideas that they will illustrate.

Then the group can assign a sequence of panels to each member. Suggest that students design the panels as a "grown-up" Big Book so that they can more easily share their completed work with the whole class.

✦✦✦ Literature Link ✦✦✦

Alliteration Explain that the story of Beowulf was first told in lines in which many words began with the same sound, and that this device is called *alliteration*. Write some examples of alliterative lines on the chalkboard for students to say aloud. (Point out that the lines don't have any end rhyme; in early Anglo-Saxon days, rhyme had not yet been developed as a poetic device.)

1. Beowulf bade brave knights to battle with him against
Grendel, that gruesome, ghastly ghoul all soaked in gore.

Invite interested students to write and read aloud some alliterative lines of their own to tell about Beowulf's adventures.

◆ **See the Annotated Bibliography on page 107 for related books your students will enjoy.**

The Many Roles of a Knight

1. A **knight** was a *nobleman*, born or accepted into a noble class. How was Beowulf a noble?

_____
_____
_____

2. A **knight** was a *vassal*, who promised to serve a lord or king. Whom did Beowulf serve?

_____
_____
_____

3. A **knight** was a professional *warrior*. His whole life was dedicated to fighting. How did Beowulf show that he was a professional fighter?

_____
_____
_____
_____
_____
_____
_____

4. A **knight** was also a *lord*. He gave parts of the land he had received from *his* lord to *his* vassals, who promised in turn to serve the knight. In the story, who are Beowulf's vassals?

_____
_____
_____
_____
_____
_____
_____

KNIGHT THOUGHTS: In your opinion, what was the best part of being a knight?

_____
_____

Beowulf

The Building of Heorot

ing of the Danes, Hrothgar was greatly respected by all the knights who served him. How glad they were that they had pledged their loyalty to him rather than to some other king! For whenever Hrothgar's knights rode off with him to battle, they knew they would return victorious. With Hrothgar-the-Mighty leading them, they were sure to gain treasures and perhaps even the rights to new lands. For Hrothgar was generous, and he was true to the promise he made to his knights: to repay their loyalty with the spoils of victory.

Soon Hrothgar himself had gained immense wealth through this constant warfare. He decided to use much of

his wealth to build a huge hall, or stronghold, which he would name Heorot (hāʹ rōt). "At Heorot," he said, "I shall entertain my knights with feasts and music. In my great hall, we shall listen to the troubadours as they sing us stories of heroes. Best of all, Heorot will be strong enough to protect us from our enemies."

For months and months, workers labored with shovels, hammers, and chisels to build Hrothgar's hall, mound by mound. On the day when Heorot was completed, the gate was thrown open and the knights and all the court entered the stronghold. They were awed by its size and delighted with the feast Hrothgar had readied for them. What a pleasure it was, too, to hear the songs of the troubadours, for many of the songs told about Hrothgar himself and his brave company of knights.

As the night and the festivities wore on, the company grew weary. They fell asleep on benches placed about the hall. Hrothgar retired to his own room, leaving 32 of his bravest warriors to guard his guests.

Who could have guessed then the savage scene that dawn's light would reveal? For when the servants entered the great hall with breakfast, not a soul was left there. The walls were splattered with blood, the floors were deep in puddles of gore. The horrified servants rushed to wake King Hrothgar.

The king surveyed the scene of carnage, then quickly noticed a clue: Giant, bloody footprints led from the hall and out the castle door. With his servants close behind, Hrothgar followed these bloody footprints through shadowy marshes and through wolf-haunted forests. On the king went as the prints led down a windy hillside,

across a field of huge, treacherous rocks, and finally downward along a stream, to where the stream flowed into a deep, dark pool that opened on to the stormy sea. There the bloody footprints stopped. Yet rivulets of blood burbled up through the lake.

"I know now that my brave knights lie dead deep in this lake!" moaned Hrothgar. "This can only be the work of Grendel! Grendel has returned!"

The Monster Grendel

Now who was this Grendel who had done such a savage deed? Grendel was a gigantic monster, part human, part devil, part animal. In olden days, long before Hrothgar's reign, Grendel had roamed freely in the marshes, fields, hills, and villages, destroying and devouring all whom he met. Because Grendel was evil, it had taken a person of great goodness to conquer him. This good person was a magician, who through his magic was able to send Grendel to the bottom of the lake, to live forever there in water caves with his monster mother and with other evil creatures. For centuries, Grendel

and the other monsters had been contained there in the deep waters by the magician's spell. Now it seemed the spell had been broken or had worn out. Grendel once again was free to ravage the land.

In Hrothgar's mind, there was no doubt: Grendel would return to land to seek more human victims. Hrothgar said, " I will ask ten more of my loyal knights from lands all around and place them in Heorot to keep watch for this odious creature and kill him!"

The ten knights loyally answered Hrothgar's call and came to Heorot to feast and listen to music—but most of all to watch for Grendel and slay him. Alas, their steadfastness came to naught. The monster broke into Heorot, killed and bloodied all who were there, and carried their lifeless bodies off to his gloomy water caves. All, that is, except for the troubadour, who managed to hide himself in a dark corner.

This musician was too terrified to continue living in Denmark, and he fled to part of Sweden called Jutland, the land of the Geats. In the court of Hygelac (hē jē läk´), the king of the Geats, the troubador

sang a tragic song relating the fate of the knights who stayed at Heorot. All those who listened were spellbound and horrified by this awful story. And one among them, Beowulf, decided that he would conquer Grendel.

A Young Hero

Beowulf was King Hygelac's nephew and much beloved by his uncle. At the time he heard the minstrel's song about Grendel's hateful deeds, Beowulf was probably about 18 years old. Whatever gave this young man the idea that he could conquer a gigantic, centuries-old monster who spent most of his time underwater? Well, Beowulf was sure of his powers because he had already fought beside his uncle in many battles and had returned home victorious. Just as important, Beowulf had proved himself to be a swimmer of superhuman endurance. This is the way it had happened:

Some years before, Beowulf had entered a swimming contest with Breka (brā´ kə), one of the lords in Hygelac's court. Carrying their weapons, the two young men plunged into the sea. For five days and nights they swam side by side, undaunted by the foaming waves that swelled about them. But then a tempest arose that churned the sea into whirlpools and waterspouts. Beowulf and Breka were separated in the storm, and Breka, struggling to survive, finally made it to shore. But Beowulf was caught up in a current that dashed him up against jagged cliffs. As he clung there desperately, angry mermaids and sea monsters called nixies began to attack him. Clutching the rocks with one hand and using his weapons with the other, Beowulf killed all these creatures.

Waiting onshore throughout the storm, King Hygelac, along with Breka and others of his knights, saw the bodies of the monsters wash up on the beach. The men thought that the storm had killed the monsters and sadly concluded that Beowulf, too, had died in the turbulent ocean. How delighted the king was then when Beowulf reappeared! To reward him for his valor, Hygelac gave his nephew his own precious sword, which was named Nageling (nä´ jə ling).

Beowulf Goes to Heorot

No wonder then that Beowulf felt sure of his ability to slay Grendel, the loathsome beast who was terrorizing Hrothgar's people. He embarked with fourteen of his most valiant knights and sailed to Denmark. Coming ashore, Beowulf was at first challenged by Hrothgar's coast guard, who did not know whether he was an enemy or a friend. But when Beowulf explained his purpose, he and his men were escorted with honor to Heorot.

Although Hrothgar was impressed by his visitor's strength and reputation, he begged him not to undertake this perilous mission, for the king was convinced by now that no one could withstand Grendel's onslaughts. But Hrothgar soon saw that Beowulf was determined. The king bowed to the young man's wishes and left him and his brave band of warriors at Heorot, first ordering that they be served a sumptuous feast. In his heart, the king sadly felt that this would be the very last meal Beowulf and his men would ever eat.

A long night of feasting made Beowulf's men feel happy and secure. So too did the words of their chief, who told them to go to sleep without fear, for he would guard and protect them from Grendel. The knights fell into a deep slumber. Only Beowulf stayed awake, ever watchful for Grendel, and thinking about the fight he knew was to come. And as he stood watch, it occurred to him that Grendel could never be conquered with spears, swords, or lances. The monster could only be overcome by hand-to-hand combat. So Beowulf

laid aside his shield and the mighty sword Nageling, and waited in the darkness for the beast.

Would this beast never come, thought Beowulf, as night began slowly to fade into dawn? Then he heard the loud tread of the monster, and heard the iron bolts of the door being wrenched away, and felt bitter-cold air flood the hall as the door was ripped apart and Grendel entered.

Before Beowulf could even rise and meet the monster, Grendel had already killed the fourteen valiant knights. But even as he reached for Beowulf, Grendel sensed that he had met his match. As man and monster grappled in the darkness, Heorot itself rocked and groaned in the violence of their blows. Finally Beowulf was able to grab one of Grendel's gigantic arms and—giving a mighty tug—pulled the arm from the creature's body. Howling in pain, Grendel fled from the hall, stumbling back bleeding to his underwater home.

Beowulf stood triumphant for a moment, then hung Grendel's arm from a beam on the the ceiling of Heorot. When morning came and

Hrothgar and his men entered the Hall, this was the sight they saw: the fourteen knights dead, but Beowulf gleeful in victory, and the immense arm of Grendel hanging as a trophy high above their heads.

A Celebration and an Awful Surprise

Overjoyed that his lands and people were now free of Grendel, Hrothgar ordered a great feast for the victorious Beowulf. Wealtheow (wel´ thou), who was Queen of Denmark and Hrothgar's wife, was so impressed with the young man's achievement that she pledged him in a special way. Touching her lips to a cup of wine, she then offered the cup to Beowulf, who—feeling deeply honored by this beautiful woman—drank the wine til the cup was dry. Queen Wealtheow then gave Beowulf a gold ring and a necklace so famous that it had a name: Brisingamen (bre sin´ gä mən).

As the banquet drew to a close, Hrothgar's warriors fell asleep peacefully in the Great Hall, knowing that the mortally wounded Grendel would never again return. Even the king's best friend, Askher

(äs´ skär), fell into a deep and dreamless slumber in the huge room. Then Hrothgar escorted Beowulf to a quiet, curtained area of the hall, where the young man could finally rest after his mighty battle with Grendel.

But peace does not always come so simply. Grendel had a mother, and she was as monstrous as he was; yet though she was a monster, she had a mother's tears. Maddened by her son's defeat and saddened by his slow-bleeding death in the gloomy sea cave to which he had returned, Grendel's mother crept into Heorot that night. She wrested her son's arm from the beam on which it hung and took it away into the darkness, back to the sea cave, along with Askher, whom she killed in vengeance.

Grendel's mother had moved stealthily, and so it was not until morning that Hrothgar and Beowulf discovered what had happened during the night. King Hrothgar wept bitterly at the loss of his best friend. He and Askher had grown up together, shared secrets, fought side by side in many a battle, and consoled one another in hard times.

Seeing the king's tears, Beowulf vowed to revenge this third grisly assault against Hrothgar. But even the young hero was aware that this new battle would be far more dangerous than the first. For this would be no land battle: to conquer Grendel's mother, Beowulf would have to dive into the sea and challenge the monster in the deep, dark recesses of her watery caverns.

With dread, Beowulf, Hrothgar, and Hrothgar's loyal knights approached the rocky shores of the horrible pool. The blood of Askher flecked the shore. Beowulf said, "Keep watch here. I can swim

underwater for two days. If I am not back by that time, then know that I am dead." Then, grasping the sword Nageling, Beowulf dived into the churning waters.

The pool was deeper than Beowulf had imagined. Downward he swam, until the darkness enveloped him and he could not even imagine where the bottom was. Slowly, however, a phosphorescent light began to gleam, and Beowulf knew then that he was nearing the cave of Grendel and his mother. Dreadful monsters rose up to clutch him, but Beowulf killed them with Nageling and swam on.

Suddenly a current like a sucking force swept him into the slimy cave where Grendel's mother lay in wait, tending to her dying son. At the sight of Beowulf, she rose up and clasped him in a death grip. The waters churned fiercely as Beowulf sought to escape her clutch and overcome her. Finally, with one thrust of Nageling, Beowulf killed the monster. Then, floundering back into the recesses of the cave, Beowulf discovered the dying Grendel and mercifully dispatched him with another strike of Nageling.

But this strike was the end of Nageling. For the blood of the monsters was so hot that it melted the sword blade, and only the hilt remained.

More than two days had passed, and Hrothgar and his men, faithfully keeping watch on the shore, saw the blood surfacing on the water. Since Beowulf had not returned, they could only conclude that the blood must be his. But then the hero surfaced, jubilantly carrying the heads of Grendel and Grendel's mother.

There was much joy in Denmark at this second victory of Beowulf. The hero was loaded up with treasures by the Danes, who were grateful to him for rescuing them from evil. And when Beowulf returned to his home in Jutland and to the court there of his uncle, King Hygelac, more honors and wealth awaited him. Beowulf's eyes shone with pride at his accomplishments. But in his heart he said, "Before I die, I shall do still greater deeds!" ♦

How Arthur Became King

STORY SUMMARY

This retelling deals with the infancy and boyhood of King Arthur. As his part of a bargain with Merlin, King Uther Pendragon allows his infant son Arthur to be removed from the royal castle at birth and to be raised instead far away by Sir Ector. This proves to be a wise move, for soon King Uther's reign is overthrown by rebellious knights, and his kingdom falls into disarray. To encourage unity, Merlin and the Archbishop summon the warring knights to Canterbury, where there appears a mysterious sword embedded in an anvil and stone. Arthur, now a teenager, pulls the sword free, and thus establishes his right to be King of all England.

The mysterious and exemplary King Arthur has fascinated troubadours and poets throughout Europe for more than a thousand years. *Mysterious*, because his real identity and even his actual existence are still debated. He may have been a leader of the early A.D. 500s who ousted German invaders from Britain. *Exemplary*, because his reign—real or not—was characterized by unity and civility in a heretofore barbaric land. It is probably the latter characteristic that kept Arthur a hero for so many war-torn centuries. Stories about Arthur were among the very first printed after the invention of the printing press in the late 1400s.

BUILDING SOCIAL STUDIES
BACKGROUND

1. Preview—Using the Poster: Students will better understand the story if they realize that religion and a belief in magic coexisted in the Middle Ages. To highlight this, ask students to find the cathedral and notice its shape from above (a cross). Point out that this structure was one of the largest in the town, and that its shape

reflected the Christian faith professed by most people in Europe at that time. Then introduce the subject of alchemy. Explain that alchemists represented much of the "science" of the age; they strove to find what they called the philosopher's stone, some element that would enable them to turn base metals into gold.

2. Leaders In discussing *Beowulf*, students probably noted the superhuman abilities of legendary people. Before reading about King Arthur, students can expand on this concept by brainstorming a list of characteristics they'd like to find in the "perfect" leader, then note as they read any ways in which Arthur lives up to this ideal. You might make notes during this discussion to refer to in the Social Studies Activity on page 25.

A SUGGESTED READING STRATEGY

Asking Questions Students can adapt the glossing strategy they practiced in reading *Beowulf*. Here, have them focus on asking direct questions of the characters in the story of Arthur.

First, list the major characters: King Uther Pendragon; Merlin; Queen Igraine; Sir Ector; Sir Kay; Arthur; the Lady of the Lake. (You may also wish to list minor characters: the Duke of Tintagil; the Archbishop; a warring knight.) Ask students to jot down some why-when-what-how questions they'd like to ask these characters as they read the story. Provide some examples of questions:

♦ King Uther, how did it feel to give up your son?

♦ Merlin, why did you want the baby to be raised by someone else?

Explain to students that these gloss questions will be useful when they plan their interview sessions (see below).

AFTER READING

Suggest to students that they "think as historians do" by trying to separate fact from fiction in stories like this one that tell about ancient times. A chart like the one below, which you can copy on the chalkboard, will help them organize their information. Have students cull the story for events and statements that fall into the three categories.

Probably True	Might Be True	Couldn't Be True
Examples: Warlords fight over a woman.	A royal baby is raised away from home.	A magician knows who will win a battle.

STUDENT ACTIVITY

♦♦♦ Interviewing the Story Characters ♦♦♦

Interviewing provides readers with an opportunity to delve into motives and cause-and-effect relationships. The process also helps students to build the concept that tales of the Middle Ages were transmitted orally, with variations in each retelling.

A good way to carry out this activity is to first divide the class into groups of five or six students, each group comprising an interviewer and the story characters they select as interviewees. Ask groups to imagine that the story characters they've chosen are gathered for a talk show. Instruct groups to add to their gloss questions to build a list of start-up questions the interviewer will ask the guests. Provide time for groups to practice their interview shows before they present them to the class.

After all the interview shows have been presented, discuss the different questions and answers and the different insights they bring to understanding the story.

ADDITIONAL ACTIVITIES

✦✦✦ Social Studies ✦✦✦

Power and Authority The stories of Arthur and of King Hrothgar in the *Beowulf* epic provide an opportunity to discuss an important Civics question: Where do people get the authority to make and enforce rules? Students probably already have noted the power that lords of the Middle Ages had over their vassals. You can firm up students' insights with the diagram below, after introducing and discussing the following definitions:

Power: The ability to direct something or someone.

Authority: The power that people have the right to use because of custom, law, or the consent of the governed.

In the Middle Ages, Power and Authority Came From Custom:

Power: Might Makes Right	Authority: Inheritance or Magical Choice
Hrothgar defeats other warlords.	Arthur pulls a magic sword out of a stone.

Explain to students that there are many variations of the power diagram above, and that democracy as we know it today in the United States and as shown in the second diagram, below, is a very recent development historically.

In a Democracy, Power and Authority Come From Custom and Law

People-Power: Choosing Representatives, Individual Rights	Authority: Representatives Creating and Enforcing laws about Taxes, Crime, or Education.
Examples: Elections; Freedom of Speech	Example: Passing a bill in Congress

Ask students to brainstorm modern-day examples of authority and power from law or customs. For instance, by custom the captain of a sports team makes decisions for the team. By law, crossing guards can direct traffic. By custom and law parents have authority to direct and control their children. Governors of states have the authority to carry out and enforce laws, because this power was given to them by the people who elected them.

To help students understand how the power of medieval lords was based on might-makes-right rather than on the authority given to them by the governed, you might use and discuss these comparative examples of power without authority:

♦ A neighborhood bully forces younger children to give up their lunch money.

♦ A robber holds up a bank.

Students might also get into a "if-I-were-King-or-Queen" mode by discussing how a good, all-powerful ruler like the fabled King Arthur might use his power to make life better for ordinary people. Ask students to debate this question: Would you like to live under the rule of a tyrant who might be supremely kind, or take your chances with someone the people have elected?

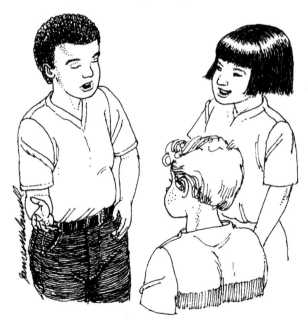

Writng a Poem About King Arthur Share with students the background information on page 22 about how the story of King Arthur has enchanted writers down through the ages. One thread in all the stories tells that even after the king's death, his story will be honored, and that perhaps he will even come back to rule as "the Once and Future King." You might read these lines of Alfred, Lord Tennyson from *The Passing of Arthur*, in which the aged king recollects the last incident described in the story in this book:

> "Thou remembrest how
> In those old days, one summer noon, an arm
> Rose up from out the bosom of the lake,
> Clothed in white samite, mystic, wonderful,
> Holding the sword—and how I row'd across
> And took it, and have worn it, like a king;
> And, wheresoever I am sung or told
> In aftertime, this also shall be known."

Encourage interested students to write their own poems based on an incident in the story. Partners or groups may wish to work together to retell all the major incidents in poetry form.

♦ **See the Annotated Bibliography on page 107 for related books your students will enjoy.**

How Arthur Became King

There was once a king named Uther Pendragon. He was fierce and stubborn, determined to get whatever he wanted, even if he had to fight for it. And fight he did, leading his vassals into battle against neighboring rulers, capturing castles and land and serfs.

Yet, there was something he could not win, and that was the love of the lady Igraine. She was the true and faithful wife of the Duke of Tintagil, and she lived in the Castle Terrabil. No matter how plaintively and sincerely King Uther Pendragon begged her, Igraine would not leave her husband. And so the

mighty king, defeated by love, asked his adviser, Merlin, to help him.

Perhaps you've heard of Merlin before. Some people say he was simply a very wise man. Others say he was a magician. Which tale is true? History is a mystery! In either case, Merlin was a person of great influence, and here is what he said to Uther Pendragon:

"You must go wage war against the Duke of Tintagil. Yes, yes! I know he has an army as powerful as yours. But I guarantee his army will fall and the duke himself will die, leaving Igraine a widow and thus free to marry you. BUT . . . this will happen only if you make me a solemn promise: You must promise to give me the first son who is born to you and Igraine."

Uther Pendragon made this strange and awful promise, and everything happened as Merlin said it would: the duke's army was defeated, the duke perished in battle, and Igraine mourned for him in the tower of Castle Terrabil. Yet she was able to dry her tears rather quickly when the King came to the castle and asked her to marry him. She accepted, became Queen

Igraine, and seemed very happy with her new husband.

In time, a baby son was born to the royal couple, and no sooner had they named him (Arthur!) than Merlin arrived to see that the king kept his part of their bargain. Merlin said, "Wrap the baby in cloth of gold and deliver him to me tonight at the castle gate. I shall take him to the castle of Sir Ector. There the child shall be raised as if he were Sir Ector's own, alongside Ector's son Kay, who shall be like a brother to your babe." And Uther Pendragon did exactly that, as Merlin directed.

As Arthur was growing up peacefully far away in his foster home, his real father began to suffer great military losses. Rebellions wracked Uther Pendragon's land, and when the king and Igraine died, evil, warring knights divided up the kingdom and treated the common people cruelly. The world seemed thrown back into a savage time, a time without peace and unity.

Old Merlin (he was *very* old but seemed to keep on going) saw all this and was deeply troubled. Off he went to the Archbishop of Canterbury and issued another of

his famous directives, which went this way:

"Archbishop, you must send for all the knights in the land, even the dreadful warring ones, and order them to come here to Canterbury to pray at Christmas. As an added incentive, tell them that there will be a tournament with prizes on New Year's Day. There never was a knight who would turn down a chance to joust!"

The Archbishop was as mesmerized by Merlin as Uther Pendragon had been long ago. He did as the old magician ordered, sending out the message to every noble family in every castle all around. Indeed, this message was delivered to Sir Ector, who set out at once for Canterbury, along with Arthur and Kay.

Arthur was still a squire and only about 13 years old. Kay was now *Sir* Kay, having been knighted just the year before. He was a forgetful sort of knight, however, and left his sword at home. How could he participate in the tournament without it?

"Brother Arthur," said Sir Kay, "ride back to the castle and get my sword for me. We will ride on to Canterbury and meet you there."

Arthur turned back on this errand quite willingly, though there were many miles to retrace. He loved his brother and looked forward to seeing him win at the games. In riding back to the castle however, Arthur missed some of the excitement at Canterbury. For when the knights arrived there, a strange and wondrous sight greeted them in

the churchyard: a huge block of stone loomed against the church wall, and set in the stone was a huge anvil, and set in the anvil, its point downward and its shining hilt upward, was a magnificent sword. And strangest of all, engraved on the hilt of the sword were these words: *Whoever pulls out this sword from the stone and anvil is a right-wise king, who shall be King of all England.*

How did this stone and anvil and sword come to be there? No one knew, but, as you might imagine, every knight who had come to Canterbury tried his hand at pulling out the sword. The idea of one king who would rule all of England seemed impossible, even ludicrous to these knights, for all they had ever known was battling one another for bits and pieces of that big island. Yet each knight thought to himself, "Who knows? The prophecy on this sword may be true." But not even the strongest among them could make the sword budge, and so the knights went off to bed grumbling and mystified.

Now we come back to young Arthur. When he returned to Sir Ector's castle to fetch Kay's sword,

not a soul was there and the gates were locked. Everyone had gone off to Canterbury to see the tournament. Arthur was rightly dismayed. His brother Kay would be a laughing-stock without his sword! Frantically Arthur turned around again and headed for Canterbury once more, saying to himself "I must find some sword or other for my brother!"

Arthur reached Canterbury in the dead of night. All was silent, all was dark. But there in the church-yard was a gleaming sword, imbedded through an anvil and a stone. "This sword will do for Kay,"

thought Arthur, and he grabbed the hilt and the sword slipped out as easily as if had been sunk in velvet. Arthur happily carried the sword to the tent where Sir Ector and Sir Kay lay sleeping. "I hope Kay will not be angry that he must use this strange sword and not his own," thought Arthur as he fell asleep.

At dawn, when Sir Ector saw the sword beside the sleeping Arthur, he of course recognized it and was awestruck! "How come you by this sword?" he said, rousing the boy. "Look here, Kay, it is the sword in the stone!"

Arthur said, "Why, father, I found it in the churchyard, stuck strangely in a stone as you said, and I pulled it out."

Sir Ector fell to his knees. "My Lord," he said to Arthur, "have you not read the words on the hilt of the sword? You will be King of all of England, as the words prophesy."

Arthur read the words on the sword hilt. He found them puzzling. How could *he* be king? Why, he was not even a knight yet! But even more puzzling to Arthur was the sight of Sir Ector bowing down to him.

"Why do you kneel to me, Father?" asked Arthur.

"Ah, lad, I am not your father," said Sir Ector, and he proceeded to tell Arthur about his real parents, King Uther Pendragon and Queen Igraine, and about Merlin's command that he be raised far away as a son to Sir Ector.

While Arthur gaped in surprise at this information, young Sir Kay began to grumble. "Frankly," he said, "I find it hard to believe that Arthur pulled the sword out of the stone at all. Maybe it fell out. Maybe another knight loosened it. I am not willing to call my younger brother *King* until he performs this feat again."

So off the three went to the churchyard, where, in the morning light, the other knights stood staring at the place where the sword used to be. They watched in astonishment as Arthur, prodded by Sir Kay, slipped the sword back through the anvil and the stone, and then—just as easily as before—pulled it out again.

This made a believer out of Sir Kay, but the other knights were greatly displeased. "This is a

shameful thing," said one, "that a boy so young can do what the mightiest baron cannot!" So the knights insisted that the boy perform the feat twice more. This he did, but the complaining continued until the Archbishop of Canterbury stepped forward.

"Do you not see," said the Archbishop, "that this boy has been sent to us by Providence to unite our land? Quit your quarreling and come into the church, where Arthur shall be crowned King of all England. And each of you shall pledge your everlasting loyalty to him."

So it was done. Arthur became king and gathered many knights about him, rewarding first those who had been loyal to his father, Uther Pendragon. And Arthur swore to them all that he would be a true king and stand for justice all the days of his life.

But there is more to this story, and another sword, too.

Remember that Arthur was very young. It took him time to learn to be a just king, and he made many mistakes in the first years of his rule. Merlin was always at his side, however, counseling and advis-

ing him. Indeed, it was Merlin who saved Arthur from a grave error. Here is what happened: Arthur struck out in an unjustified rage against a good knight, Sir Pellinore, who Arthur mistakenly thought was disloyal to him. But as Arthur angrily brandished his sword (the very same one he had pulled from the stone), it fell apart.

"How shall I rule without the sword that established my right to do so?" moaned Arthur.

"A wise and just king," said Merlin, "does not seek revenge or punish people without knowing the facts of the case. In this case, the facts are that Sir Pellinore has always been your loyal vassal, just as he was always loyal to your father. The sword-from-the-stone knew this, even though you did not, and the sword would not harm an innocent man."

Arthur understood and bowed his head in shame as he asked Sir Pellinore's pardon. And at that moment, from the lake by which they were all standing, a white-draped arm rose out of the water, holding aloft a jeweled sword. As Arthur gaped in amazement, a

the young Arthur. There are many more tales of the adventures of this amazing king and of the knights and ladies of his court. It is said that Arthur united England for many years, kept the peace, and ruled with courage, wisdom, and compassion. This is exactly the sort of king the people wanted. ♦

beautiful woman, clothed all in white, appeared at his side. She was the Lady of the Lake, and she told him that the sword was intended for his use.

Joyfully Arthur rowed to the center of the lake and took the sword, which was named *Excalibur.* The Lady then told him that this weapon had mystical powers: As long as the scabbard remained in his possession, he would never suffer a wound or a defeat.

Now you know the story of

The Dapple-Gray Palfrey

STORY SUMMARY

Blanchefleur, the daughter of a baron (in the medieval power structure, barons were second only to kings), falls in love with a poor knight, Guillaume, but cannot marry him because her father will give her in marriage only to a noble who is as rich as he himself is. Through trickery, Guillaume's wealthy, aged uncle manages to have himself selected as the bridegroom. But through the courage and persistence of Blanchefleur and the cleverness of Guillaume's horse (the dapple-gray palfrey), the true lovers are united at last. (A palfrey is a kind of saddle horse that was often used in medieval times.)

This retelling is based on a *fabliau*, or realistic story, from 12th-century France. A fabliau was generally not presented in castles to noble families, but rather sung or told by a minstrel to an audience of peasants and to an audience of the bourgeois—the merchants and shopkeepers and small landowners who were becoming a powerful group during the later years of the Middle Ages. The story is retold here in prose. The minstrel, of course, would have recited it in verse accompanied by music.

BUILDING SOCIAL STUDIES
BACKGROUND

1. Preview: The Evolution of the Castle into a Self-Contained Community. Your students probably know by now, from the description of Heorot—the castle to which Beowulf traveled—that early castles were simply a huge earthwork with one main room, protected by a wet or dry moat. Two or three centuries later, castles had developed into much larger, more complex, almost self-sufficient compounds. **Using the Poster:** You may wish at this point to discuss the castle shown on the poster.

2. Arranged Marriages Explain that young persons in noble families (especially young girls like Blanchefleur, who were considered "property") had little or nothing to say about whom they would marry. Marriage was considered not so much a union between individuals as a union between families. Parents "gave" their daughters—sometimes as young as nine or ten—in marriage to noblemen not much older whose families could match or add to the economic standing of the bride's family. These unions also established or reinforced a political and military union between the men of the two families.

♦ Suggest to students that as they read *The Dapple-Gray Palfrey* they will see how Blanchefleur and Guillaume defied this customary way of arranging marriages.

A SUGGESTED READING STRATEGY

Tableau. A tableau is a "frozen scene" from a piece of literature. To create a tableau, students have to understand the story action and the characters' feelings well enough to provide a vivid image of them for the audience.

Explain the procedure: Students "freeze" themselves into positions that illustrate a chosen scene from the story. A leader then taps a person in the scene, who speaks what the character is saying or thinking, while the other actors remain frozen. Only one character speaks at a time. The leader controls the action by tapping the next tableau figure who is to speak.

You may wish to have students form groups and choose their own tableau scenes after the story has been read. Or you can form student groups beforehand, read the story aloud, and call on groups randomly to make a tableau at the conclusion of each major scene. More than one group can take turns showing the same scene. This latter strategy is a good one for ensuring participation by students of different abilities and for encouraging different interpretations of story characters.

AFTER READING

♦ **Story Settings** Ask partners or small groups to refer to the poster to determine where various scenes in the story take place.

♦ **The Castle Community** With a larger group, or with the whole class, talk about the workers shown around the castle and how their work served the day-to-day life of the noble family. Discuss and review why so much of the castle structure and so many of its workers were devoted to protecting the people within the castle walls.   If necessary, remind students that the basic work of lords and knights during the Middle Ages was to attain property through warfare, and that castles were basically fortresses to protect a noble's family from other nobles.

STUDENT ACTIVITY

♦♦♦ Making an Illuminated Day Book ♦♦♦

To prepare students for the activity, explain that the story heroine, Blanchefleur, is unusual for her times because she knows how to read. Most lords and ladies were barely literate, if at all; and if noble families employed tutors, it was usually the boys alone who were allowed to take lessons. In addition, books were rare and precious commodities during the Middle Ages, because each one was entirely made by hand, from writing to illustrations to binding. Expensive and ornate, created by professional scribes and artists, these books were treasured by the noble families who owned them. They were often called *day books*, because each day

the reader was to ponder the story on a page.

What might have been the contents of the books that Blanchefleur discussed with Guillaume? The books of the time had varied themes. Most were sober and reverential, each page containing a prayer or a summary of a moralistic story or a brief recounting of heroic deeds of long ago. Some books were merry, however, with descriptions of plants and animals or of daily work in and around the castle. Whatever the contents, however, the book was sure to be lettered perfectly and illustrated gorgeously and extravagantly, with colorful pictures accompanying each page and brilliant illuminated capitals and scrollwork.

Ask students to use the story, the poster, and preceding tales to brainstorm some subjects that Blanchefleur's books might cover. List these on the chalkboard. Examples are life inside a castle, deeds of King Arthur and Beowulf, morals from animal fables, and the rules of chivalry and courtesy.

Next, distribute copies of page 40 so that students can get an idea of the beauty and intricacy of the designs found in medieval manuscripts. Talk about the geometrical patterns, the repetition, the spirals, scrolls, the plaits that intertwine like ribbons. All of these were in color, of course. You might also stress that any animals, plants, or people shown in the designs had something to do with the contents of the page on which they appeared.

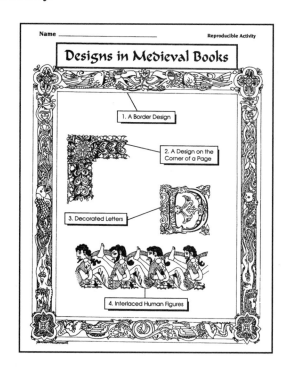

Encourage students to color the designs, to adapt them for their own day books, and to make up designs and illustrations of their own. This is an activity for which you'll want to provide drawing paper and an assortment of writing and art materials for the final products. However, caution students to make their preliminary designs and plans on scrap paper. Some students will want to make their own complete books, while others may enjoy working with a partner or small group to make individual pages.

ADDITIONAL ACTIVITY

♦♦♦ Social Studies/Literature ♦♦♦

A Woman's Life In spite of its fairy-tale feeling, *The Dapple-Gray Palfrey* presents a fairly accurate view of the life of noblewomen during the Middle Ages. Ruled by men, confined to manor or castle, and responsible for the smooth running of the household, the daughters and wives of nobles seldom had a chance to make their own choices or to go adventuring in the wider world. After discussing this concept, ask interested students to retell this story or a traditional fairy tale presenting the heroine as an up-to-date, modern young woman with a mind of her own. Students can write and illustrate their stories or act them out with classmates.

♦ **See the Annotated Bibliography on page 107 for related books your students will enjoy.**

Name _____

Designs in Medieval Books

1. A Border Design

2. A Design on the Corner of a Page

3. Decorated Letters

4. Interlaced Human Figures

The Dapple-Gray Palfrey

 a humble minstrel new to your town, will tell you this story of the dapple-gray palfrey, which was told to me by another, who heard it from someone else. I believe the tale to be true, though it happened some years ago. It is a story worth remembering, for it will help you appreciate the patience, loyalty, intelligence, and courage of women.

But let us start with the knight in this story. His name was Guillaume. He was far from wealthy, for the rent from his lands brought in only about two hundred pounds a year. Yet Guillaume had a good heart and a happy nature. What he lacked in wealth he

made up for in honor and gallantry, for he was skilled at jousting and won almost every tournament he entered. Wealth did not mean much to Guillaume, anyway. The only possession he truly treasured was his horse, a beautiful and clever dapple-gray palfrey, which was the envy of every knight in the land.

Now let me tell you of the lady in this story. Her name was Blanchefleur and she was the daughter and only child of a wealthy and powerful baron, who lived in a magnificent castle many leagues from the humble castle of Guillaume. Besides his money—which he valued greatly!—the baron prized his daughter. Not only was Blanchefleur beautiful, and accomplished at music and sewing, she would also someday inherit all his wealth. So the baron was determined that he would give her in marriage only to a man who was as rich and powerful as he was.

Ah, what a sad life Blanchefleur lived in the meantime! Imagine it: From the time she was born, her father never let her go beyond the castle walls! Why not? He was afraid that she would see some penniless fellow and fall in love and run away.

He was afraid that her great beauty would tempt some worthless man to kidnap her, or that she would be held for ransom, or that she would get lost in the forest, or . . . . You name it: The baron made many excuses for keeping his daughter a captive in her own castle.

Well, dear listeners, as you might imagine, almost every knight for miles around had come at one time or another to pay his respects to the baron and to beg to marry Blanchefleur. Each suitor was stunned by her beauty and thought, "Ah, I would have a wife who was not only rich but also wonderful to look at."

But, "You're not rich enough!" the baron would declare. "What makes you think I would give

my child to a knight who had no great fortune?" So the land was full of disappointed suitors.

Now, the only knight who had not visited the baron this way was Guillaume. He had never seen Blanchefleur. And yet, he had managed to fall in love with her, and she with him. How could so strange a thing have happened? This is where the dapple-gray palfrey comes in.

Some time ago, Guillaume had become curious about the far-away captive princess. So, mounting his palfrey, he journeyed to her castle, but not by the usual, well-trodden road. No, indeed. Horse and knight made their own new, narrow path through the thick, dark forests, a little path that led from Guillaume's gate to the outer wall of Blanchefleur's castle. In this wall, there was a tiny crack, just big enough for Guillaume and Blanchefleur to whisper through. And this is what they had done for many months: Guillaume and the horse traveled on the secret path, Blanchefleur waited inside the wall, and then the two young people talked together through the crack about books they had read, tourna-

ments, and so forth, and eventually about their growing affection for one another. For though they had no idea what the other looked like, Blanchefleur fell in love with Guillaume's merry nature and respectful manners, and Guillaume fell in love with Blanchefleur's wisdom and sweetness.

There came a day when Blanchefleur said to the knight, "There is no man except you whom I wish to marry, Guillaume!"

"And I wish no other wife but you, Blanchefleur," answered Guillaume. "But marriage between us is impossible. Your father would never allow you to wed a man as poor as I am."

"I've thought about that," said Blanchefleur, "and here is what you must do. I know you have an old uncle, a very rich baron, who lives in a mighty castle not far from this one. Your uncle and my father are friends and comrades from many years back, and my father has great respect for him. You must go to your uncle and explain our situation to him. Beseech your uncle to visit my father here and plead your case for you. Ask your uncle, further, to

give you five hundred pounds, so that he can truthfully impress upon my father that this is your yearly income. I know my father will then accept you as his son-in-law under these terms. But promise your uncle that you will return the five hundred pounds as soon as you and I are wed."

"What a brilliant idea!" responded Guillaume. "I shall do as you suggest and go to my uncle immediately." And off the young knight rode, with his heart and hopes high, feeling blessed to love such a clever woman.

Guillaume's old uncle received him hospitably, even though this baron was so bent with age that he could barely hobble and so hard of hearing that he said, "Eh? eh? eh?" many times before he understood what Guillaume was asking. But finally the old man said, "Why, of course I will do this favor for you, nephew!"

Guillaume was overjoyed, of course. "I am in your debt forever, Uncle," he said. "And while you are doing this great errand for me, I shall ride off to the tournaments. For though I have no wealth to offer Blanchefleur, I can at least share with her the honors I win at jousting."

Ah, listeners, there is deceit where we least expect it! When Guillaume's uncle visited Blanchefleur's father, he did not plead his nephew's case, but instead asked to marry Blanchefleur himself! And, horror of horrors, the baron agreed to the request!

"Indeed, you are just the sort of man I wish to give my daughter to," said the baron. "You are an old and trusted friend, and more important, you are as rich as I am, so that my daughter and any children she may have will be heir to your lands as well as to mine! I will tell my daughter to prepare for the wedding immediately!"

Poor Blanchefleur! When she learned her fate, she screamed, then wept, then said that she would rather die than marry such an old wretch, then wept again. "What injustice is this, Father," she cried, "that you should hand me over to someone I have not a bit of love for?"

"Love? Love?" said the baron. "What has love to do with marriage? Get your gown ready, for the wed-

ding will take place tomorrow morning in the little chapel that lies on the other side of the forest, on your bridegroom's great estate."

Then leaving his despairing daughter, the baron went off to arrange the wedding procession. All his old nobles would accompany him and Blanchefleur to the chapel, each riding a beautiful horse and wending their way through the forest down the broad road to the chapel.

Now, as it happened, there were not enough fine horses in the stable to accommodate this big wedding procession, so the baron, as was his right as lord of the land, commanded that knights who were his vassals send him their finest steeds to use for the occasion.

"Especially," said the baron, "we will need the best horse in the kingdom to carry my daughter to church."

"Ah," said the stable master, "that would be the dapple-gray palfrey that belongs to Guillaume! How such a poor knight ever came by such a fine horse nobody ever figured out, but all of us know that palfrey is the best there is!" So, the baron sent a servant to fetch the dapple-gray palfrey.

Now recall, listeners, that Guillaume had been off to the tournaments, and thus knew nothing about the foul treachery of his uncle or about the impending wedding of his beloved Blanchefleur. Thus, when the baron's servant came to borrow the horse and explained simply that the baron needed it for a ceremony, Guillaume handed the palfrey over with a merry heart, saying to himself, "This is the least I can do for my future father-in-law!"

At the baron's castle that evening, there was much feasting and entertainment, and all the elderly lords enjoyed themselves until they nodded off to sleep. Even the servants, drunk with wine, dropped into early slumber, snoring their way into the night. Only Blanchefleur stayed awake, pacing the floor of her room and crying.

The moon rose. A full, bright moon, lighting up the castle windows and splashing light in the courtyard and beaming into the face of the groggy watchman. "What, ho!" said the befuddled fellow. "It's dawn already!" So, thinking it was daybreak, the watchman roused the

baron and all the visiting lords and their servants and bade the stable master get the horses ready to ride to church.

As for Blanchefleur, she was too distressed and angry to care what time of day it was. Her servant led her to the dapple-gray palfrey, she mounted it, and with her servant following behind on his own horse, she followed the rest of the wedding party down the broad forest road. "What a sad fate awaits me!" she thought. "Wed to a man I despise, never to talk again with my beloved Guillaume, perhaps never even to know what he looks like!"

Now, remember that it was still nighttime, and the old fellows leading the wedding procession were still sleepy. One by one they nodded over their horses' necks and started snoring again, as did their servants. Even the servant who followed Blanchefleur and the palfrey went back to sleep. On the horses trod, down the familiar forest road, heading for the chapel . . . all except the dapple-gray palfrey. For he had come to the narrow, secret path along which he had so often carried Guillaume on all those visits to Blanchefleur's castle. And the palfrey turned onto that little path, leaving the procession and carrying Blanchefleur into the heart of the dark forest.

Yes, of course Blanchefleur was a bit alarmed. Remember, she had been cooped up in a castle all her life and so had never been in a forest before. Moonlight played tricks with shadows, strange sounds emanated from thickets and ponds, leaves and branches cracked and crackled underfoot. "I don't care," thought Blanchefleur. "I would rather die in this gloomy place than marry that old man."

Gently, gently the palfrey carried her on until, when the real dawn broke, Blanchefleur found herself at the gate of another castle, a run-down sort of place, not grand

at all. The watchman in the tower saw her approach and ran to his master, who—as of course you have guessed!—was the brave knight Guillaume.

"Master!" said the watchman. "What a sight there is outside! A beautiful lady dressed in such finery, and she is riding your dapple-gray palfrey!"

Guillaume ran to the gate to see this sight. As soon as Blanchefleur began to explain who she was, he recognized the voice of his beloved. And when Guillaume answered her, Blanchefleur knew too that fate had been kind after all.

"Have you a chapel here? Have you a priest?" asked the happy young woman.

"Yes and yes!" answered Guillaume. "Let us marry immediately!" And so, as the sun rose in a bright and cloudless sky, the young lovers were wed.

Far away, outside the old uncle's chapel, the baron and all the members of the procession had finally awoken. There was great distress when no one could find the bride. Servants were sent back along the road to find her and to inquire at every cottage and castle. But of course when Blanchefleur was eventually found, she already had a husband. Though her father was angry at this turn of events, there was nothing he could do about the matter. A wedding is a wedding.

"Well, let her live with that poor, ragtag knight," the baron grumbled. But when the baron died some years later, Blanchefleur inherited his estate. And when Guillaume's uncle died, that estate came to the nephew. So it was that this couple was in the long run blessed with a great fortune as well as with their constant love for one another.

So that is the story of the dapple-gray palfrey, as it was told to me. And I believe it, for who would not agree that the patience and ingenuity and loyalty of a woman can work great wonders? ◆

The Story of the Little Bird

STORY SUMMARY

In the orchard of a rich and ruthless ruler, a nightingale sings songs that preach a kind and chivalrous way of life. The man, annoyed by these homilies, traps the bird and plans to kill it. The bird wins its freedom by promising to tell its captor three secrets that will lead to profit. The "secrets" turn out to be simple, commonsense advice that the man has been too ignorant and greedy to follow. After teaching the man the error of his ways, the bird leaves the orchard forever, and the land around withers.

Like *The Dapple-Gray Palfrey*, this story was probably popular with minstrels. The story of Blanchefleur reflects old, romantic notions about knights and ladies. However, *The Story of the Little Bird* reflects the common people's realistic view of what was happening as the old feudal and manorial systems fell apart and peasants could no longer count on the economic and political protection of the landowner.

BUILDING SOCIAL STUDIES BACKGROUND

1. Preview—Using the Poster: Students can discuss the shops, signs, and buildings shown in the town clustered around the cathedral outside the castle walls. What

goods and services are offered to ordinary folks in town that duplicate those provided in the castle?

Discuss how the signs and the town itself show a growing independence from the lord of the manor, as well as new ways for ordinary people to make a living.

2. The Decline of Knighthood In the days of Beowulf and King Arthur, knights were committed to military service for their lord and thus were often away from home and engaged in battles. Through the centuries, however, knights found it wiser politically to stay home and direct the defense of their own strongholds, and more profitable economically to tend to the running of their vast estates. Knights who would no longer take part in distant battles now had to pay a war-tax called *escuage* to the lord. With money raised this way, and through the actual selling of land, honors, and titles to men who had not inherited them, kings were able to hire soldiers—a whole new way of raising troops. During the Crusades, vast armies of foot soldiers set out who had no part in the old feudal system of homage and fealty. They fought for pay, for the love of adventure, and for the promise of a share in the plunder. As mercenaries, these soldiers hired themselves to the highest bidder—often changing sides and fighting in the same war for opposing camps.

3. The Manorial System Feudalism was basically a relationship between a knight and a lord. The manorial system was a relationship between the knight and the peasants who worked his land. These peasants were at first serfs, virtual slaves who went along with the property and who depended on the lord for protection. As far-flung wars called their masters from home, many serfs simply ran away to make their living freely as best they could. As hard currency came into use in Europe, some serfs were able to save enough to buy their freedom. At the same time, this growing money economy led to the development of a middle-class of tradesmen and craftsmen who could support themselves quite well. As ordinary people became increasingly disillusioned by the excesses of the nobility, and as they became more independent of the noble class, the manorial system slowly began to weaken.

♦ After sharing this background with students, ask them to look for clues in the story that show the changing attitude of common people toward wealthy and powerful landowners.

A SUGGESTED READING STRATEGY

A Story Chart The chart on page 53 can help students focus on the essentials of the story and thus increase their comprehension and analysis of it. In turn, this will help students write their own moral tale. Distribute copies of the chart and discuss the headings and how they can guide students as they read. Suggest that students complete the chart with a partner or small group.

After Reading The follow-up discussion of completed story charts will enable students to share insights and generate prewriting ideas.

STUDENT ACTIVITY

♦♦♦ Writing a Tale with a Moral ♦♦♦

Students may wish to write stories independently or with a partner. Beforehand, discuss with the class how the story chart on page 53 can help them plan their own story with a moral. Explain that tellers of this sort of tale usually start out knowing what moral they're going to teach; writers, then, should first focus on the chart headings **What is this story really about?** and **Values brought out in the story**. With these decisions made, they can more easily move on to developing story characters and a story problem that will lead to a solution and to the moral.

Encourage students to use these aspects of *The Story of the Little Bird* as a model:

♦ One character is unusually good or or wise or both, while the other is unusually evil or cruel.

♦ There are elements of magic or fantasy in the story.

Suggest that students use the poster to get ideas for a story setting. The class might also brainstorm characters from different stories who can appear in their original ones, such as Merlin and Grendel, or the evil uncle from *The Dapple-Gray Palfrey*. Some writers may prefer to cast their story with modern-day folk in today's world.

Presentation of finished stories can take various forms: an illuminated and illustrated book to add to the collection students made for *The Dapple-Gray Palfrey*, a read-aloud story, a dramatic presentation, a radio play. Whatever the form of the tale, ask the audience to use the Story Chart as a guide to what to listen for. Then use the Story Chart as a guide for class discussion of the students' tales and suggest they use the chart for any revisions they wish to make.

ADDITIONAL ACTIVITY

♦♦♦ Social Studies ♦♦♦

Adults and Children You can use *The Story of the Little Bird* to launch students on a discussion of the relationship of adults and children in the Middle Ages. Students can then make charts comparing medieval childhood with childhood in their own culture today.

First, you might have students brainstorm two lists: a list of recreational activities they participate in only with peers, and a list of recreational activities they participate in with parents or other adults. Then explain that in the Middle Ages there was no such separation: Everyone—children and their parents alike—listened to and enjoyed moralistic and guessing-game stories like *The Story of the Little Bird*; and indeed—as evidenced by medieval art and literature—played the same games, such as leapfrog, blindman's bluff, tag, and hide-and-seek; listened avidly to the same legends; and took part in the same songfests and plays.

Why was this so? Depending on the comprehension level of your students, you may wish to discuss with them the following points:

♦ In the Middle Ages, life expectancy was short by our standards. Infant mortality was common. Adults were considered old if they lived to be forty. (Some students may wish to research the medical and scientific knowledge and practice of those days and compare them with more modern developments in those fields.)

♦ Children who survived birth and disease were immediately considered adults and given adult chores according to their station in life. Children married in their teens or before. Young females, whether serfs or nobility, tended households and raised their own children, while the young males learned a trade or went off to battle.(Many a sixteen-year-old member of the nobility was put in charge of whole armies.)

♦ Thus, much of European society in the Middle Ages was essentially in the hands of adolescents. Heavy as their political and economic responsibilities might be, they were still filled with the rambunctiousness and playfulness of youth and found outlets in the games we today might consider "just for kids."

After the discussion, students can form groups and work together to make a contrast/comparison chart titled **Growing Up in the Middle Ages,** with columns headed **What Might Have Been Fun About It** and **What Might Have Been *Not* Fun About It.** Bring groups together to discuss their charts. Ask the class how their work on the charts has helped them to better understand the behavior of medieval adults and children.

♦ **See the Annotated Bibliography on page 107 for related books your students will enjoy.**

Name _____

• STORY CHART FOR •
The Story of the Little Bird

Main Characters:
_____
_____

Words and Phrases That Describe the
Characters: _____
_____
_____
_____
_____
_____
_____
_____

Problem(s):
_____
_____
_____

Solution(s): _____
_____
_____
_____
_____

Setting:
_____
_____
_____
_____
_____
_____
_____
_____

What is this story really about? _____
_____

Values brought out in the story: _____
_____

The Story of the Little Bird

here was once a very rich man whose fief was so large and fair that people tell about it even to this day. The manor house itself was bright and beautiful to see, and all the fields and farms around were filled with crops. The most pleasant part of it all was an abundant orchard, where trees were always heavy with fruit of various kinds and a shining fountain splashed cool water up in plumes.

Everyone in the land—rich and poor alike—loved to walk in this orchard, not only because it was so fair but also because it was the home of a nightingale, who sang there twice a day.

And the nightingale's songs had words to them, which gave instructions about how to live wisely and kindly. One day the nightingale might sing: "All you knights who seek for glory in foreign lands, remember this: You must look about you at your neighbors who are poor and needy and share your riches with them." On another day the nightingale might sing: "Do not be envious and wrathful, but always courteous and kind."

How strange it was that such a fine land and orchard and bird should belong to this particular rich man. He had not built the place himself. No, indeed! The kingdom had been built long ago by a fine and perfect knight, who had given it to another knight for services rendered. And this knight had given it to still *another* knight, and so on through the years. Each time the land changed hands it was to a lord far less chivalrous and compassionate than the one before, so that the kingdom and its people found themselves increasingly ruled by unworthy masters. And this rich man of whom we speak at present was the worst of the lot—careless, selfish,

and often cruel. He was not satisfied with plundering other men of his rank or riding off to wars. When he came home, he would tax the peasants even more heavily to pay for his battles and conscript their young sons to serve as common soldiers in his army.

Now this lord, as you might imagine, was not happy to hear the songs the nightingale sang, for the messages made him feel guilty. "I will put an end to this troublesome bird!" he finally said to himself. So one bright morning he set up a snare in an orchard tree, and when the little bird began to sing, the lord pulled the net tight around it and then roughly plucked it out.

"Ah, my dainty fellow!" laughed the lord. "That's the last song you will sing, for I'm going to take you home to the cook, and he will make you part of my supper!"

"Well, my lord," said the nightingale, "I will make a very poor meal indeed, for I weigh only an ounce as you can tell, which is hardly one bite for such a lusty appetite as yours. Better that you should set me free. And in return I will tell you three secrets that men of your noble

sort seldom know and from which you will profit greatly."

"Tell me the secrets, and I will let you go," said the rich man.

"I would be foolish to trust someone who had caught me in a snare!" responded the bird. "You must release me first."

The man held the bird and pondered. The idea of profit appealed to him finally, of course. "Oh, very well," he muttered, releasing the nightingale. "Now tell me the three secrets!"

The bird flew to a branch far overhead and began to preen its ruffled feathers, while the man paced anxiously below, saying, "Come,

come! The secrets!"

"Very well," said the nightingale at last. "Here is the first secret: *Don't believe everything you hear.*"

"What kind of a secret is that?" demanded the man. "Why, that's simply an old saying that everyone knows to be true! You had best come up with two secrets that are better than this silly one, or I'll have you trapped and put your feathers in my hat!"

"Listen well to the second secret then," said the bird calmly. "It is this: *Do not regret what you have never lost.*"

"By my faith!" stormed the lord. "Why do you plague me with these silly sayings? What man is stupid enough to regret what he never lost? Do you take me for a fool?"

"Indeed, my lord," said the bird, "you are no more foolish than any other rich man. But listen well to my third secret, for whoever understands it will never be poor. The secret is this: *What you hold in your hands, never throw between your feet.*"

"Again you taunt me with sayings that every child knows!" the man ranted.

"Ah," said the bird, "but if you knew the third secret you would never have let me out of your hand!"

"You speak the truth about that," grumbled the lord. "But at least I know the meaning of the other two secrets."

"But the third secret is worth more than the other two," said the nightingale. "For if you had held on to me and taken me home and cut me open, you would have found inside me a huge jewel, three ounces in size . . . a jewel with miraculous powers. For whoever holds it may wish on it and have everything his heart desires—kingdoms, power, wealth beyond measure—all that sort of thing."

At these words, the rich man fell to the ground, raving that he had been wretchedly tricked, cursing the bird for its vile deceptions, and wailing over the lost opportunity to own such a magic jewel. The bird watched from its high refuge in the tree, and if a bird can smile, this bird did.

Finally, when the man's wailing had finally quieted into sobs, the bird said to him, "You miserable churl! Could you not tell when you held me in your rough hands that I weigh only an ounce? How could I then have inside me a jewel that weighed *three* ounces? To my mind, you seem to be a stupid fellow who does not know the meaning of my first secret at all!"

Still the man wept and gnashed his teeth. "And look at you now," the bird continued, "groveling on the ground and bawling over something that you never had at all. Obviously, you do not know the meaning of the second secret either. Not one of the three secrets do you know, these secrets that you proclaimed even children hold in their memory!"

With these words, the nightingale left the orchard forever, never to sing there again. And with his departure the trees and flowers withered, the fountain ceased to flow, and all the fields and farms grew brown and dry. So it was that the greedy man lost all of his fair land, and the people on it lost their livelihood. For so it is in life, that one man's greed and cruelty can bring disaster on his own head and on the innocent heads of others. ♦

The Three Thieves

STORY SUMMARY

This is a comical tale, bordering on slapstick, about a thief who "reforms" but can't fully escape his former companions until he successfully gets back the bacon they stole from *him*. Woven into all the hilarity and hijinks, however, are some glimpses of the hard-scrabble life of the poor during the Middle Ages.

BUILDING SOCIAL STUDIES BACKGROUND

1. Dwellings of the Poor. Through reading the first five stories and doing some of the attendant activities, most students now have a pretty good idea of how castles were constructed and how people within these castles

lived. Ask students to be alert to clues in *The Three Thieves* that tell what the homes of the poor, outside the castle walls, were like. As the story is being read, direct attention to:

> ◆ The paragraph in which Dame Maria tells her husband about the visitors (page 65). The house was made up of one room, in which the family stored and prepared and ate food, kept tools, and slept. (The houses were generally windowless and had only one doorway.)

♦ The sentence in which Haimet and Barat break into the house. It was easy to dig a hole in a cottage wall (page 66). (These tiny, one-room houses were framed with widely spaced timbers, between which \was packed *wattle*, a combination of mud and straw.)

2. The Forest. Ask students to note the settings of the story: the forest and the cottage of Maria and Travers, which is on the forest edge. Until the latter years of the High Middle Ages, most of Europe was covered with primeval, old-growth forest. That is, the forest was everybody's "backyard." While it could be threatening, dangerous, and gloomy, the forest was also a resource that provided firewood, wood for building, game animals, berries, nuts, etc.

3. Thieves. Explain that thieves abounded during the Middle Ages, preying mostly upon the poor. So when going about at night, especially in the forests, sensible people traveled with companions and carried torches. There were few precautions a poor homeowner could take, however. As students will see, thieves could easily break into cottages. While there was no equivalent of a modern-day police force to protect ordinary people, gross and constant offenders might eventually be caught and hauled before a magistrate. The usual punishment was death by hanging, as the first paragraph of the story indicates.

A SUGGESTED READING STRATEGY

Read Aloud To prime students for playmaking, you'll probably want to emphasize the dialogue in the story. To do this, you might read the tale aloud yourself, or share the reading among student readers.

Directed Reading You can ask other students to carry out different play-preparation steps as they listen to the story or read along silently:

♦ List the names of the story characters.

♦ List the most important actions or events.

♦ Imagine scenery: Make notes about or draw rough sketches of the two settings (forest, cottage).

♦ Make notes about props—objects you think the actors will definitely need—for the play.

AFTER READING

Encourage students to share ideas about what makes the story funny, about the moral it lightly teaches, and about the mental pictures they formed of actions, characters, and settings. You may also wish to have students discuss the character of Travers. Is he a good guy, a bad guy, or a little bit of both? (Call attention to his motive for leaving a life of thievery.) How do you predict he will behave in the future?

STUDENT ACTIVITY

♦♦♦ Planning a Dramatic Performance ♦♦♦

Ask students who have made directed-reading notes to share their ideas with the class, then discuss how these ideas might be incorporated into a dramatic performance. From this discussion, students can decide what form their presentation will take. In addition to considering a fully scripted play with scenery and costumes, students might consider readers' theater, improvisation, a taped or radio play, or the following form from the Middle Ages.

The Minstrel and the Mimes Minstrels were the traveling storytellers and news distributors of the Middle Ages. Unlike the privileged and comfortable troubadours, who lived within a castle and were the servants of a lord, minstrels were poor men who went from town to town and depended for their livelihood on postperformance handouts from the audience. Many minstrels traveled alone, singing their story songs and accompanying themselves with a lute.

However, many other minstrels gathered together and traveled with a group of young actors and acrobats—usually homeless or runaway children—who would pantomime the story as the minstrel told it, sometimes interspersing the pantomime with spoken lines, or exclamations. Your students might enjoy recreating the story in this authentic way. It's a method that allows natural groupings of five students: the minstrel and the four story characters. Suggest that the class sit in a circle around each group as it performs, just as long-ago townsfolk gathered outside around the minstrel and his troupe.

In between performances, talk about how actors interpret roles in different ways, what is especially fun about each group's presentation, and how audience reaction helps or hinders actors.

ADDITIONAL ACTIVITIES

♦♦♦ Music ♦♦♦
"Till Eulenspiegel": A Medieval Story Set to Music

Introducing the Music Richard Strauss's tone poem "The Merry Pranks of Till Eulenspiegel" (1894) is based on a medieval legend about a prankster/thief, who, according to tradition, lived in Brunswick, Germany, and died about 1350. As is the case sometimes with particularly colorful thieves, such as America's own Billy the Kid and the James Brothers, Till's crimes became romanticized over time until the thief became reinterpreted as a sort of counterculture hero. Peasants liked hearing about Till because his practical jokes and often brutal tricks were played on merchants, priests, and sometimes noblemen—all members of a ruling class that usually despised the poor.

Before playing the music, read the descriptive notes accompanying the recording that tell what Till is doing in each section of the tone poem. Suggest that students listen for the way the mood and instrumentation musically illustrates each of Till's adventures. Some students may enjoy making sketches of the events as they listen.

Follow-Up After talking about the music and the story it tells, ask students to compare the mood of the tone poem with the mood of *The Three Thieves*. Both are quite rollicking and humorous. As a class or in small groups, students can discuss people's *realistic* feelings about thieves and outrageous practical jokers (e.g., terror, disgust, a desire for revenge or justice), then respond to the questions "Why do people often make jokes and funny stories about what they fear?" "What are the differences and similarities between medieval and modern reactions toward thieves and their victims?" "What protections against thievery do people have today that were unavailable in the Middle Ages?"

♦♦♦ Literature Links ♦♦♦

Trickster Tales *The Three Thieves* is an example of a trickster tale. Students who have read other trickster tales, such as those about Anansi the Spider or Coyote and Raven, might get together in small groups to determine how the stories are alike: characters play practical jokes on one another, tricksters generally go unpunished (at least within the framework of the story), and there is usually a moral, which may be stated or unstated but obvious. Groups may enjoy writing and illustrating their own trickster tale, set in a medieval background.

Fairy Tales Remind students that most European fairy tales developed during the Middle Ages. Invite students to brainstorm a list of fairy tales in which the forest setting is important, as it is in *The Three Thieves*. Discuss why this setting is so prevalent in fairy tales, and why it so often a scary place.

♦ **See the Annotated Bibliography on page 107 for related books your students will enjoy.**

The Three Thieves

 here were once three thieves who went about the countryside robbing church folk and common people. Now, two of these thieves—Haimet and Barat—were brothers and very skillful, for they came from a long line of robbers, most of whom had already been hanged. The third thief, Travers, was new at the business of stealing. A poor man, he had fallen in with the brothers only recently. He was hoping to learn from them, to gain a bit of money, and then to return home and live an honest life with his beloved wife.

One day, as the thieves rested in the forest, Haimet

pointed to a magpie nest in the branches above them. "Friends," he said, "a clever thief could climb this tree, reach into the nest, and steal the egg on which that magpie sits without the bird ever knowing it!"

"Truly, no one in the world can do such a thing!" said Barat.

"Just watch me!" whispered Haimet. And stealthily he climbed the tall tree, so quietly that not even a leaf trembled. Reaching delicately into the nest, he removed the egg, and the magpie never rustled a feather. Triumphantly, egg in hand, Haimet descended to the ground.

"By my faith!" exclaimed Barat. "That's a daring deed. But I wager you can't put the egg back again without disturbing the bird."

"Oh no? Then watch again," said Haimet. "I shall put the egg back without even cracking it, and the magpie will never know."

So up clambered Haimet again. But, unseen by him through the thick branches, Barat climbed stealthily behind him and with cunning, agile hands removed his brother's breeches without Haimet even knowing it. Thus, with his breeches gone, Haimet replaced the egg and

once again descended.

"You see?" Haimet boasted. "No one has fingers as quick as mine!"

"Your fingers may be quick, but your brain must be slow," said Barat. "For you can't even remember to put your breeches on in the morning!"

"Indeed, I have breeches!" said Haimet. But then he looked beneath his tunic and saw that his legs were bare!

The two brothers laughed and jostled with one another over this trick. But Travers, the third thief, was disheartened by it. "I can never be as quick-fingered and clever as

you two are," he said. "The life of a thief is not the life for me. I'm going home, where I shall earn my bread as honestly as I can."

Haimet and Barat laughed as Travers left them and headed out of the forest. "Once you're in the company of thieves, you can never get away," Barat hollered after him.

Travers closed his ears to this. He went home to his wife, Dame Maria, who greeted him joyfully and forgave him for his wandering ways. "Look here, husband," she said, "I have even fattened the pig so that we may enjoy a Christmas feast of bacon."

So Travers killed the pig, sliced it into bacon, and hung the bacon from the rafters of the little house to dry. Then he went out into the woods to gather branches and sticks for the fire.

Now, as you might expect, Haimet and Barat had followed Travers and had hidden themselves outside the house. While Travers was away gathering firewood, the brothers went into the house and spoke cordially to Dame Maria, who sat working at her spinning wheel.

"We are friends of your hus-

band," said Barat, "and have come to wish him a good holiday."

"But since he is not here," said Haimet, "we trust you will give him our message." And, after lingering a while and looking all around and making admiring comments about the bacon on the rafters, they left.

When Travers returned, Maria told him about the visitors. "I didn't like them at all!" she said. "How they stared at everything in the room! Our little fireplace, our bedstead, our ax and knife and reaping hook, the wooden bowl in which we knead bread, and even the bacon!"

"Ah, wife!" sighed Travers. "I know who these men are! They are the two thieves I was stupid enough to join for a while! And I suspect they will return tonight and try to steal the bacon."

"Then we must hide it!" said Maria. "Let's cut it down from the rafter hooks and put it under the bread bowl." So this is what the fearful couple did. Then sadly they went to bed.

But Travers was restless, unable to sleep, with thought that

thieves were hanging about outside. Up he got and went out into the moonless night to seek them out and force them away.

And while he was away, Haimet and Barat quickly cut a hole through the wall of the cottage and crawled in to get the bacon. But of course it was no longer on the rafter hooks where they had seen it. How to find it? Barat crept over to the bed where Maria lay deep in sleep. "Good wife, good wife," whispered Barat in a voice much like Travers's, "I am so muddled with the day's events that I forget where we hid the bacon."

"It's under the bread bowl," mumbled Maria, never realizing that this was the voice of a thief.

Barat and Haimet quickly picked the bread bowl up, stole the bacon, and fled into the forest, Barat carrying the heavy load of meat on his shoulders.

When Travers returned to the house, Maria awoke and said, "Ah, husband, how confused and tired you must be, to have forgotten where we hid the bacon! I trust you found it under the bread bowl, as I told you."

It didn't take Travers long to figure out that the two thieving brothers had played this trick and stolen the bacon. Off he ran into the forest, where the darkness of that night made it almost impossible to see what lay around one. In due time, he caught up with Barat, who—because of the heavy weight he carried—lagged behind Haimet.

"Look here, " said Travers, imitating Haimet's voice, "you have carried that load of bacon long enough! Let me carry it now."

Barat gladly hoisted the burden over, and Travers took it and turned hastily homeward, stumbling through the dark forest. But it was not long before Barat caught up with Haimet and demanded to know where the bacon was.

"But you have it!" said Haimet.

"No, *you* have it!" said Barat. Then he thought but a second and said, "Ah, no, *Travers* has it! He tricked us, but I shall get our prize back."

Quickly Barat tore a sleeve from his shirt and wound it around his head like a scarf a woman might wear. He ran through the gloomy

forest until he caught up with Travers. Then, imitating Maria's voice, Barat said, "Dear husband, I've looked high and low for you! Let me carry the bacon home quickly, while you continue your search for these dreadful thieves!"

Quite deceived, Travers handed the bacon over. The gleeful Barat ran off with it, soon catching up with his brother. And after a fruitless search through the dark forest, Travers returned home.

"I couldn't find the thieves," he said to Maria, "but at least you have brought the bacon safely home."

"But, indeed I haven't got the bacon at all," said Maria. "I have never left the house since it was stolen!"

"Then Barat and Haimet have it still!" said Travers. He dashed back into the forest again. He would never have found the thieves, were it not that a gray dawn was now breaking. Through the hazy mists, Travers saw a curl of smoke rising and smelled the scent of roasting bacon; for Haimet and Barat had decided to cook their feast right away.

How could Travers wrest the bacon from these two clever thieves? He must think of a trick! This he did: Silently climbing a tree over their heads, he took off his shirt and waved it above them. In a gloomy, ghostly voice he said "I am the spirit of hanged thieves. Woe unto you sinners who take food from the mouths of the poor!"

Haimet and Barat looked up in horror. "It's the voice of all the thieves who've gone before us!" cried Haimet.

"Leave the bacon and flee!" shouted Barat. The brothers ran from their campfire, leaving the half-cooked bacon on the coals.

Travers came down from the tree, grabbed the bacon, and ran home with it. "Maria," he said, "let us finish cooking this bacon quickly, and then enjoy it, even though Christmas is not yet here."

But of course, Haimet and Barat soon discovered that they had been tricked by a shirt waving in the mist and made their way back to Travers's house. Bursting in, they demanded a share of the meal.

"A third for each thief!" said Haimet.

So that even though Maria had raised the pig and Travers had made the bacon, they were forced to hand over two-thirds of the food to the thieving brothers. After feasting, Haimet and Barat left and never again returned. And Travers was left for all his days to think of the wisdom in the old proverb: "Bad is the company of thieves." ♦

Robin Hood and the Widow's Sons

STORY SUMMARY

A widow tells Robin Hood that her three sons are to be hanged for the crime of poaching, killing deer on the king's land. Robin, determined to rescue the young men, buys a beggar's ragged clothes and in this disguise approaches the sheriff and tells him he would like to be the hangman. The sheriff agrees to this. When Robin mounts the gallows, he blows on his bugle, thus summoning his own men. They rescue the widow's sons and hang the sheriff.

The earliest written mention of Robin Hood is in 1377, in *Piers Plowman*, by which time he was already a culture hero wrapped in oral legend and celebrated in ballads. The story of Robin Hood probably has some basis in fact. He may have been one of the last Saxons, still holding out in the 12th century against Norman invaders. He has also been associated with Randle, Earl of Chester, and may have been the earl himself. In that case, Robin would have been a member of the nobility who left his life of privilege to aid the poor.

BUILDING SOCIAL STUDIES BACKGROUND

1. Preview—Using the Poster: Students can find large areas of dense forest shown in the poster. Ask students to tell why Robin Hood lived in the forest instead of in town. (The forest was a good hiding place for outlaws.) Students can verify their ideas as they listen to and read the ballad.

2. New Heroes for Old Most students will recall that in the early Middle Ages, the heroes of song and story were kings, especially the ideal knight, as represented by King Arthur. As the era grew to a close, such heroes remained popular among the nobility, but Robin Hood and others like him had become the heroes of the "common people." Robin Hood represents the concepts and values of the ascendant farmers and tradespeople. He redistributes property, taking from the rich and giving to the poor. He loves the forest (the greenwood) and the free life and is an accomplished archer. He is adventurous, witty, generous, and protective of women. While he is religious he loathes corrupt monks and friars. He abides scrupulously by laws that do justice to ordinary people, but rebels against laws that oppress them, such as the poaching law, and law-enforcers.

3. Property Rights and Poaching *Poaching* is the killing of game animals that belong to someone else. In the Middle Ages, land belonged to nobles, and forests were stocked with deer, boar, pheasants, and other animals that the nobility hunted for sport as well as for food. As the ballad of *Robin Hood and the Widow's Sons* indicates, it was a crime punishable by death for ordinary people to kill these animals; and yet peasants poached constantly, because they were usually hungry. It was the responsibility of the sheriff to protect the landowner's rights; so, in the Robin Hood ballads, Robin and the sheriff are usually protagonist and antagonist, representing the people's evolving ideas of common justice and the injustices of the manorial system.

A SUGGESTED READING STRATEGY

Reading Aloud Distribute copies of the ballad, and suggest that students number the 21 stanzas so that they can get an idea of what a stanza is (a division of a poem characterized by the same number of lines and the same meter and rhyme scheme). Students will have fun reading the ballad aloud themselves after you read it to them first. In doing so, you can point out the following features that will enhance both comprehension and oral reading:

♦ Ballads usually have refrains, or repeated lines. In this ballad, the refrain is in the first two lines of stanzas 2, 6, and 15. Refrains usually appear to signal a change of scene or characters, as here where Robin meets first a widow, then a beggar, then the sheriff. The line in italics in the refrain is a standard "nonsense line" that serves as an additional signal. Remind students that ballads were sung; some students may be able to give examples of refrains and nonsense lines in popular songs of today.

♦ To keep the rhythm of the lines consistent, end words must frequently be pronounced in a way we're not accustomed to. Usually this pronunciation reflects the way English words were actually said in the late Middle Ages, as in stanza 4 where *die* is pronounced <u>dee</u>, or in stanza 6 where the accent on *highway* is on the second syllable, as it is on *money* in stanzas 17 and 18.

♦ Some of the words in the ballad will also be unfamiliar to students. Suggest that students underline some of these words as they listen and read along. Afterwards, they can find the word meanings, such as for <u>boon</u> and <u>fallow</u>, in an adult dictionary, or discuss the probable meaning of them, such as for <u>bags of bread</u> (bread bags made into clothes); then write the meanings in the margin, using the gloss for <u>list</u> and <u>white money</u> as examples.

AFTER READING

The Story in the Ballad In a class discussion, ask volunteers to summarize the story in sequence. After sharing the background material (above), talk with students about why the common people of the late Middle Ages enjoyed this story and why members of the nobility were not so fond of it. Also, use this opportunity to review the oral nature of "news" in olden times: Major events were passed along by word of mouth, and the minstrel, traveling from town to town, was often the "journalist." Students can discuss how actual events, when transmitted orally, often change a lot in the retellings and through time until they sometimes take on the aura of legend, so that it's hard to separate fact from fiction. (The children's party game of "Telephone" is a good comparison.)

News Stories in Rhyme To prepare students for writing their own News Ballads, talk about how rhyme and rhythm not only are fun and entertaining, but also in the Middle Ages served as a memory device both for the singer-minstrel and for the listeners who wanted to pass the tale along. As a preview of student News Ballads, you might take part of a current news event and ask students to recast it in rhyme. For example, if a community is currently debating the site of a landfill, the story could be introduced this way:

> O where shall we put the garbage and trash,
> The bottles and paper and cans?
> "O put it wherever you like," said the folk,
> "As long as it's not on *my* lands."

A Student Read Aloud Invite students to work together to practice reading parts of the ballad aloud. For this purpose, you might divide the ballad into four sections (stanzas 1–5; 6–10; 11–14; 15–21) and assign a section to four groups. Suggest that groups identify lines they wish to read chorally, and lines they'll divide up for solo reading. After groups have practiced and have their section down smoothly, the ballad can be presented in sequence to the class.

STUDENT ACTIVITY

◆◆◆ Writing News Ballads ◆◆◆

In this activity, students can work alone or with a partner or small group to write a ballad based on an event in the news. Make a variety of newspapers and news magazines available as an idea source. Before students begin, you may wish to review with them the characteristics of ballads. (They tell a story, have stanzas with predictable rhyme and rhythm schemes, and use refrains.) Students can present their ballads in a variety of ways: reading them aloud alone or with a partner; pantomiming the action with classmates as a narrator reads the ballad; presenting them as a TV news broadcast, in which "modern" reporters speak in poetry instead of in prose; copying the ballads and publishing them as a *Ballads for Our Times* newspaper; illustrating copies of the ballads for a class book; setting the ballads to music and singing them.

Wherever appropriate, encourage students to memorize all or parts of their ballads so that they can get the "feel" of being a medieval minstrel.

ADDITIONAL ACTIVITY

♦♦♦ Social Studies ♦♦♦

Limited and Unlimited Governments Stories about Robin Hood reflect the waning, toward the end of the Middle Ages, of *unlimited government*, in which there had been no effective way of restraining those in power. (If your students have done the activity on pages 25-26, they might review now where power and authority can come from.) Here is an opportunity for your students to explore not just what the Civics terms *limited government* and *unlimited government* mean, but how the concepts affect their own day-to-day lives.

The death knell of unlimited government was sounded in 1215, when nobles rose against the misused powers of King John and forced him to sign the Magna Carta, the essence of which is in this statement, which you might copy on the chalkboard: "No freeman shall be taken, or imprisoned, or outlawed, or exiled, or in any way harmed . . . except by the legal judgment of his peers or by the law of the land." What a startling concept this was 800 years ago! It established trial by jury instead of judgment at the whim of a ruler; it placed *laws* above the ruler, and made rulers themselves subject to those laws instead of above them. This began the concept of limited government.

Today, limited governments are constitutional governments, in which there are legal limits on political power. Your students can have lively discussions and debates as they grow in their comprehension of what *rights* and *laws* mean in a limited government.

Rights Using the Bill of Rights as a guide, have students brainstorm their rights as citizens of the United States, with which those in power cannot interfere, for example freedom of speech and freedom of religion. (Remind students that in the Middle Ages it was a capital crime to speak against a ruler, and to follow a religion other than Christianity was punishable by exile or death.) Help students to identify other contemporary governments that are limited (examples are Great Britain, Botswana, Japan, Israel, Chile); as well as some that are unlimited (examples are South Korea, China, Iraq, Iran). Students might discuss why people involved in democratic movements, such as that in Haiti, sometimes say they are trying to "move their nation out of the Middle Ages."

The Rule of Law In the early Middle Ages under unlimited government, "the rule of men" prevailed, that is, the rules made by king and nobles for others to follow. In contrast, under "the rule of law" people are governed by widely known and accepted rules that everyone must follow. These laws are designed to protect individual liberties and the common good. Again, have students brainstorm laws that everyone in a limited government is supposed to follow (such as traffic laws, tax laws, laws about weapons, and laws about littering or pollution) and then discuss how these laws are meant to protect individuals and society as a whole.

Students can also discuss what happened during the Middle Ages because of the lack of the rule of law: Anarchy prevailed and people suffered as knights warred with one another and land changed hands; rulers behaved in capricious and unpredictable ways; people could prey upon one another unchecked; there were no established and fair procedures for dealing with people's claims or with criminals. Encourage students to refer to *Robin Hood and the Widow's Sons* and to other tales they have read, such as *The Three Thieves*, *The Dapple-Gray Palfrey*, and *The Story of the Little Bird*, to cite other examples of injustices that occur when there is no rule of law. Students might retell parts of these stories to show how the fates of the widow's sons, the sheriff, the thieves, Blanchefleur, and the evil landlord would be different had they been ruled or protected by laws.

♦ **See the Annotated Bibliography on page 107 for related books your students will enjoy.**

Robin Hood and the Widow's Sons

 here are twelve months in all the year,
    As I hear many men say,
But the merriest month in all the year
    Is the merry month of May.

Now Robin Hood is to Nottingham gone,
    With a link a down and a day,
And there he met a simple widow,
    Was weeping on the way.

"What news? What news, thou simple widow?
    What news hast thou for me?"
Said she, "There's my three sons in Nottingham town
    Today condemned to die."

"Oh, what have they done?" said Robin Hood,
    "I pray thee tell to me."
"Oh, it is for killing the king's fallow deer,
    That they are condemned to die."

"Does thou recall, old woman," he said,
    "How thou gave me food and wine?
By the truth of my body," quoth bold Robin Hood,
    "You give me this news in time."

Now Robin Hood is to Nottingham gone,
    With a link a down and a day,
And there he met with a simple old beggar,
    Was walking along the highway.

"What news? What news, thou simple old man?
    What news, I do thee pray?"
Said he, "Three squires in Nottingham town
    Are condemned to die this day."

"Come change thy apparel with me, old man,
    Come change thy apparel for mine;
Here are forty shillings in good silver,
    Go drink it in beer or wine."

"O, thine apparel is good," he said,
    "And mine is ragged and torn;
Wherever you go, wherever you ride,
    Laugh not an old man to scorn."

"Come change thy apparel with me, old fellow,
     Come change thy apparel with mine;
Here are twenty pieces of good broad gold.
     Go feast thy brethren with wine."

Then he put on the old man's cloak,
     Was patched black, blue, and red;
He thought it no shame all the day long,
     To wear the bags of bread.

Then he put on the old man's breeches,
     Was patched from leg to side:
"By the truth of my body," bold Robin did say,
     "This man had little pride."

Then he put on the old man's hose,
     Were patched from knee to wrist:
"By the truth of my body," said bold Robin Hood,
     "I'd laugh if I so *list."

Then he put on the old man's shoes,
     Were patched both beneath and above;
Then Robin Hood swore a solemn oath,
     "It's good clothes that make a man."

Now Robin Hood is to Nottingham gone,
     With a link a down and a down,
And there he met with the proud sheriff,
     Was walking along the town.

"A boon, a boon," says jolly Robin,
     "A boon I beg of thee;
That as for the death of these three squires,
     Their hangman I may be."

*list= desired

"Soon granted, soon granted," says Master Sheriff,
   "Soon granted unto thee;
And you shall have all their fine clothing,
   And all their *white money."

"O I will have none of their fine clothing,
   And none of their white money,
But I'll have three blasts on my bugle horn,
   That their souls to heaven may flee."

Then Robin Hood mounted the gallows so high,
   Where he blew both loud and shrill,
Till a hundred and ten of Robin Hood's men
   Came trooping over the hill.

"Whose men are these?" says Master Sheriff,
   "Whose men are these? Tell unto me."
"O they are mine, but none of thine,
   And are come for the squires all three."

They took the gallows from the slack,
   They set it up in the glen,
They hanged the proud sheriff on that,
   And released their own three men. ♦

*white money=silver

The Canterbury Tales

STORY SUMMARY

In a very real sense, *The Canterbury Tales* is a story about telling stories, and also a story about the storytellers themselves. The stories are set in a frame, or context, of a larger story: Thirty pilgrims set off from the Tabard Inn, near London, to travel the 70 miles to the shrine of St. Thomas à Becket at Canterbury Cathedral. At the suggestion of the innkeeper, the pilgrims agree to amuse one another during the trip by telling stories. Included here are the Introduction to *The Canterbury Tales*, in which the pilgrims are briefly described, and three of the tales, all greatly abbreviated and retold for young contemporary readers.

1. The Wife of Bath's Tale: "The Loathly Lady" A knight who has committed a crime can escape execution only if he goes out into the world and finds the answer to the question: *What is it that women most desire?* Just as the knight is about to give up finding the answer, he meets a wretched-looking crone who says she will provide the correct response if he in turn will grant her the first thing she asks after they return to the royal court. The knight agrees to the bargain. And, in the opinion of the ladies of the court, the response is correct: *Most women desire to have sovereignty over their households and their husbands.* The old woman claims her due: The knight must marry her. This he sadly does; but after he agrees that he is lucky to have a wise and compassionate bride, ugly though she is, the crone changes into a beautiful young woman.

2. The Pardoner's Tale: "The Three Thieves" In this somber story, quite different from the humorous story of the same title on page 63, three roisterous young outlaws set out to slay Death himself, who has been taking so many people during the Plague. A strange old man, whom the thieves treat discourteously, tells them that Death is under a nearby tree. The thieves find a pile of gold there instead and exult in their good fortune. However, their greed and duplicity leads them to slay one another, thus fulfilling the old man's prophecy.

3. The Nun's Priest's Tale: "Chanticleer and Pertelote" In this merry fable, the handsome rooster Chanticleer dreams that he is captured by a wild animal. Chanticleer's beloved wife, the hen Pertelote, scoffs at her husband's fear over this dream and urges him to regain his courage and strut about the barnyard as usual. This Chanticleer does and is promptly carried away by Reynard the Fox. The rooster suggests to Reynard that he yell at the foolish humans who are in hot pursuit. As the fox does so, Chanticleer falls from his open mouth and escapes.

Geoffrey Chaucer died in 1400, leaving *The Canterbury Tales* uncompleted. The unfinished poem is about 17,000 lines long and is considered the greatest story written in English during the Middle Ages—indeed one of the greatest works in world literature. It is noteworthy because it was written in the vernacular, or common language of the people of the time (which we call Middle English), instead of in Latin or French, the traditional languages used by scholars and poets in Great Britain and Western Europe. But it is other aspects of the *Tales* that make them truly memorable and enjoyable even today:

♦ The pilgrims who tell the tales and who are presented briefly here in the Introduction show us vividly the three strata of society as the Middle Ages waned: the nobility, as represented by the Knight and his son; the clergy, as represented not only by the corrupt Pardoner, but also by the humble Nun's Priest (who acted as a chaperon for the Prioress); and the working class, both rich and poor, who were experiencing economic and social ascent by Chaucer's time.

♦ The storytellers seem to be real human beings, fleshed out by the poet not only in their appearance but also in all their human frailties and strengths. Breaking with literary tradition, Chaucer did not idealize his characters or paint them with broad strokes as stock figures. Your students will get to know the Wife of Bath, the Pardoner, and the Nun's Priest in the brief introduction to each of their stories.

♦ Not only did Chaucer have stunning insights into the character of his storytellers, but also the storytellers themselves are quite aware of what makes them tick and of why their particular stories reflect their personalities and interests. For example, the aging Wife of Bath, five times a widow, rightly claims to be an authority on the subject of her story, "What do women want?" and on another theme that runs through the tale: respect for older women. The Pardoner, as smarmy a villain as exists in literature, understands his own hypocrisy in telling a tale about the fate of greedy, duplicitous people. Nowadays we expect story characters to have this quality of self-reflection, but in Chaucer's time there was no precedent for it. Chaucer literally created this facet of literature.

♦ *The Canterbury Tales* celebrates the fun of storytelling itself. The entire opus and the individual tales within it are designed to entertain the reader and listener. Unlike other medieval tales, whatever morals exist here are what the reader perceives, not what the writer teaches or emphasizes. Your students will have fun responding to the humor in the tales, discussing how the stories reflect the personalities of the tellers, and comparing any moral lessons they construe.

♦ For writers and readers, young and old, the frame story structure of *The Canterbury Tales* provides a wonderful unity and a fine writing model. You can discuss the frame with your students after they read "An Introduction to the Canterbury Pilgrims," and ask them to be thinking about a frame within which they can tell and write their own stories later on. The frame might be a school bus trip to a distant location, an imaginary vacation they all take together, or an imaginary event such as a power failure or a storm during which they are all gathered together until the crisis has passed.

BUILDING SOCIAL STUDIES
BACKGROUND

1. Preview:—Using the Poster: Students can find a group of pilgrims wending their way along the road leading to the great cathedral town. Call attention to the condition of this "main road." Like all highways of the time, it was muddy, narrow, and rough, and wound through forests where thieves might lie in wait. For pilgrims, there was safety in numbers. Even so, the 70-mile journey from London to Canterbury took several days. Have students identify the cathedral, the pilgrims' destination.

2. Cathedrals Just as castles stood as testimony to the power of the nobility, cathedrals were evidence of the power of the Christian church during the Middle Ages. Typically, a cathedral took hundreds of years to complete. (Canterbury Cathedral was constructed between 1000 and 1400.) Explain that in the Middle Ages a cathedral was used not only as a church but also as a town meeting hall and an educational center. For religious purposes, the cathedral was not only a place of worship, but also the headquarters of a church district and the seat of the bishop or archbishop, the chief administrator of the district.

3. Pilgrimages A pilgrimage is a journey to a sacred place or shrine. An extremely popular activity during the Middle Ages, the pilgrimage is still a vital part of many religions today. Chaucer's pilgrims were going to Canterbury Cathedral to pay homage to the saint buried there, Thomas à Becket, or Saint Thomas the Martyr. Becket (c. 1118–70) was appointed Archbishop of Canterbury by his good friend King Henry. It was Henry's hope that Becket would support him in his struggle to gain the upper hand in certain disputes the Crown had with Rome. When Becket threw his support to Rome instead, the King is said to have blustered, "Will no man rid me of this meddlesome priest?" Four knights took the King seriously and murdered the Archbishop in the cathedral. Thomas à Becket was popular with the people and their faith was more important to them than was Henry, a decidedly unpopular king. So the assassination did not sit well. Becket was canonized and his grave became a shrine for pilgrims from all over England.

A SUGGESTED
READING STRATEGY

Building on Prior Knowledge Knowledge charts such as the one on page 87 provide a way for students to pool previous learnings on a topic and then share new knowledge they've gained. As a prereading activity, students can work together to summarize what they've learned so far about people of the Middle Ages. Ask the class to brainstorm a chalkboard list of the kinds of medieval people they've met and studied in this book's activities and stories and in related titles. Then individually or with partners, students can refine and note ideas in the first column of the Activity Sheet on page 87, the column headed **Prior Knowledge About People of the Middle Ages**. Sample entries:

> **KNIGHTS, early Middle Ages:** owed allegiance to warlord kings
> **LORDS:** big warriors; fought for, gained, or lost new lands
> **NOBLEWOMEN:** usually subordinate to men; big household responsibilities

Next have students form four or five study groups. Explain that each group will read and discuss the Introduction, toward the purpose of filling out the second column on the Activity Sheet, *New Knowledge About People of the Middle Ages.* The Introduction (especially the capitalized words) along with poster study and any background information you wish to share (page 82), are particularly rich sources of facts and follow-it-up hints about people of the late Middle Ages. Encourage groups to follow-up through further research in dictionaries and encyclopedias as they complete their charts.

Groups can stay together to read and discuss the three tales. Suggest that groups make notes about story features they especially like or don't like.

AFTER READING

Sharing Charts Ask reading groups to come together and share and discuss the notes they've made on their Knowledge Charts. You may wish to make a master chart based on entries that the class feels inspire special insights into the Middle Ages. Conclude the discussion by inviting students to tell how the activity itself has helped them learn. What happens to your own knowledge when you pool it with the knowledge of your classmates? How does discussing other people's ideas help you to clarify your own ideas?

Discussing the Stories and the Tellers Using the information that follows the story summaries on page 79, and the character highlights in the mini-introductions to the three tales, you can phrase questions that will spur lively class discussions. Examples are "Why do you think the Wife of Bath chooses to tell a story about marriage?" "The Wife of Bath was old by standards of the Middle Ages. What part of her story shows how she wishes to be treated as an elderly lady?" "What is the Pardoner like as a person? Which character or characters in his story does he resemble? Find some evidence that lets you know that the Pardoner knows how evil he is."

STUDENT ACTIVITY

♦♦♦ Writing Frame Stories ♦♦♦

Page 81 describes frame stories and suggests some frames your students might consider for this class project. Invite the class to brainstorm alternative settings, or frames, in which a group of people might decide to tell stories to amuse one another.

A. After students have voted for the frame they like best, they can appoint a classmate to write the Introduction, modeled on the one on *The Canterbury Tales*, which describes the setting. You might at this juncture mention that the

"I" in the *Canterbury* Introduction is supposedly Chaucer himself; the class-appointed introduction writer might similarly adopt this first-person stance as she or he writes about how the narrator and the storytellers happen to be gathered together.

B. Explain to students that they will write, independently or with a partner, a story that fits within this agreed-upon frame. Review with students the common components of the three Canterbury Tales they've read: (1) The stories are fun. They have lively plots and characters. (2) The stories reflect the interests and beliefs of the storytellers. For example, the Nun's Priest's tale reflects ideas that churchmen of the Middle Ages believed: Danger lies in the outside world, and don't trust the advice of your spouse. Encourage students to think about stories, old or new, that express feelings and ideas they agree with.

C. At this juncture, you might also tell students that many of the Canterbury Tales were based on old stories that Chaucer had heard (mostly in his visits to Italy) and then embellished with his own unique insights, character development, and wit. Following this pattern, your students can base their own stories on plots and characters in traditional fairy tales or stories of the Middle Ages, or make up original stories of their own.

D. Ask students to write their stories and then review, edit, and revise them with a writing partner. You may wish to review stories with individual writers to help them clarify how their tales answer the criteria in **B.**, above. As part of this conference, some students may enjoy composing a brief self-introduction, like those in *The Canterbury Tales*, to explain why they choose to tell this particular story.

E. Ideally, publication of the stories will be oral, for that's the way Chaucer's pilgrims told them, jogging along toward Canterbury. Reader's Theater is an ideal format: To establish the frame for the audience, the appointed student can read or improvise on the Introduction he or she has written. Then storytellers can come on one by one to introduce themselves and relate their tales. After some class practice and discussion, your students may wish to present their frame stories in other classrooms, in the school library, or to parents and other adults. Suggest that students tell the audience briefly about how their program was inspired by Chaucer's *The Canterbury Tales*.

ADDITIONAL ACTIVITY

♦♦♦ Social Studies ♦♦♦

Cathedral Windows Stained glass windows incorporate aesthetic features that most middle-school students appreciate: bold black outlines (formed by the window leading) and bright colors. In cathedrals of the Middle Ages, these windows illustrated not only religious stories from the Bible, but also events from popular secular tales like *The Story of the Little Bird* and from the mythology of revered rulers like King Arthur. Invite interested students to create designs for stained glass windows showing some of the medieval events and characters they've read about. Designers can use colored marking pens to make the black outlines and brilliant pictures. Students who are more ambitious might cut the outlines out of black construction paper, then cut and paste colored tissue paper to this backing to show the details of the picture. These make a great display when mounted in a sunny window. Your artists can ask their classmates to guess which stories their stained-glass designs stand for, then discuss the details in the designs that provide clues. Students can also mount their design on a bulletin board and ask a partner to help them write a story caption for it.

♦ **See the Annotated Bibliography on page 107 for related books your students will enjoy.**

Name _____

◆ KNOWLEDGE CHART ◆
People of the Middle Ages

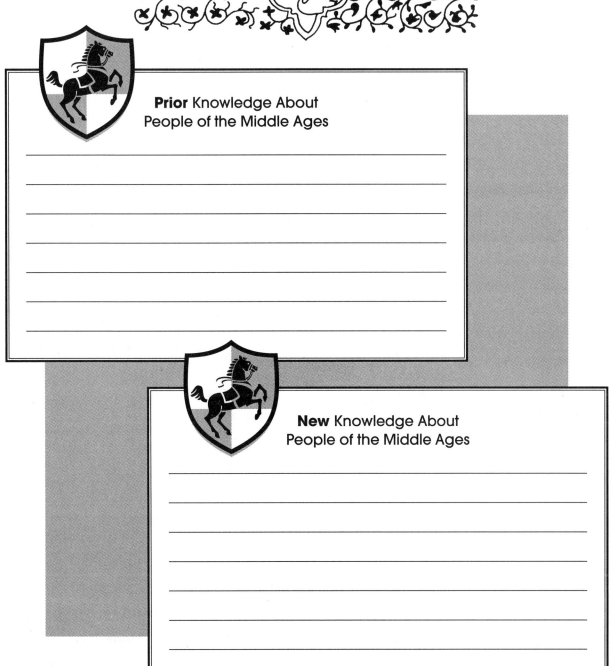

Prior Knowledge About
People of the Middle Ages

_____
_____
_____
_____
_____
_____
_____

New Knowledge About
People of the Middle Ages

_____
_____
_____
_____
_____
_____
_____

An Introduction to
The Canterbury Pilgrims

When April rain bathes the earth and makes grass and flowers grow, and when the west wind gently stirs the leaves, the little birds begin to make us merry with their songs. This is the time of year when people long to be outdoors! And in England it's the time when people journey to Canterbury to visit the shrine of Saint Thomas à Becket. He's the one we prayed to when we were sick, so it seems only right to give thanks to him now.

It was a spring day when I left London to make my pilgrimage to Canterbury.

Just south of the river Thames, I stopped for the night at a place called the Tabard Inn. What a cheerful place! There I met twenty-nine other pilgrims, all headed for Canterbury, too. We decided it would be a good idea to travel together.

Altogether, the pilgrims represented almost every kind of person you can find in England. To begin with we were honored to have a member of the nobility with us, a KNIGHT who was valiant and courteous, along with his young son—a SQUIRE—and a YEOMAN who was the knight's servant. This merry fellow was dressed all in green and carried a sheaf of arrows with peacock feathers on them.

In our group, there were several members of the clergy, too. For instance, there were two nuns, one of whom was a PRIORESS; a PRIEST who rode along with them; and a MONK and a FRIAR (neither one of whom stayed inside much to pray, but instead were always singing and drinking and looking for good company).

Then there were two pilgrims whose work was connected with the church, though you'd hardly believe it by looking at them. One was a SUMMONER. He had a horrible, fiery-red face that frightened little children. His job was to summon people to court, but when he wasn't doing that he was usually drinking

in a tavern. Then there was a PARDONER. He carried a case full of pardons he said he'd gotten from the pope, and some worthless tidbits he said had belonged to saints. He'd sell these things to simple people for high prices.

A number of rich and distinguished men were in our group, too. There were a MERCHANT, a PHYSICIAN, and a LAWYER, along with a FRANKLIN, a well-to-do landowner. The Franklin had

represented his county in Parliament and had also served as a Justice of the Peace.

With us also was a SAILOR who said he had made many people walk the plank. And there was a WIFE from the city of Bath. She had a bold, red face and wore scarlet stockings, a broad hat, and several kerchiefs wound around her head. There were also a REEVE, a MILLER, and a MANCIPLE. The Manciple made a living buying food and drink and then selling them at a tidy profit to a group of lawyers. The Reeve, a thin and sour man, took care of an estate belonging to a rich lord. He did a good job as a caretaker, but of course he, too, made a handsome sum of money in the process.

Now, our HOST was the owner of the Tabard Inn. His name was Harry Bailey, and he was a large, handsome, friendly, and talkative man. He gathered us all together and said, "You're the merriest band of pilgrims that's come by here all year! I know you'll be talking and telling jokes all the way to Canterbury. I have a suggestion for getting yourselves organized. Why don't each of you tell two stories on the way to Canterbury and two stories on the way back? I'll go along with you as a guide and also as manager of the storytelling. When we get back here, we'll vote on who has told the best tale, and the rest of you will treat that person to a fine supper! What do you say to that?"

We all agreed that our host's idea was a fine one. Of course, he stood to make a profit from serving a big supper like that, but that didn't bother us, for he was a good-hearted person and offered fine food. And so, after confirming our agreement, we all went to bed and started off together for Canterbury the next morning. ♦

The Wife of Bath's Tale

Prologue: The Knight had been the first storyteller. His tale was very long indeed. It was about courtly love and tournaments of long ago, and all of the Pilgrims thought it was quite a romantic and wonderful story, although rather long and old-fashioned.

"Now who will tell the next tale?" asked the Host as the travelers moved along the road.

"I have a story to tell," said the Wife of Bath, "and believe me, it is not romantic and outdated. It is about a real-

life question that often arises between wives and husbands, and that is *Who shall be the boss?* I'm an authority on this subject, for I have had five husbands. Three were good and two were bad. My fifth was one of the good ones, but only after I taught him that a husband should always obey his wife. Do I have your attention, so that I can tell the tale that proves this to be so?"

"Yes, indeed," said our Host. "Tell on, and we shall listen."

The Loathly Lady

Long ago, in the days of King Arthur, there was a knight who carried off a young lady against her will. Now this was such a grave crime against the law of chivalry that the punishment was death, and King Arthur was ready to behead the knight. But the queen beseeched the king to hand the knight over to the ladies of the court for judgment and sentencing.

"That sounds correct to me," said King Arthur. "For a crime against a woman should be judged by women."

The queen and her ladies called the knight before them, and

the queen said this to the knight: "Your crime is punishable by death. But I shall grant you your life if you can tell me what it is that women most desire. You have one year to find the answer, and if you swear to return within that time and come back with the answer, your neck is safe."

The unhappy knight agreed to these conditions. What else could he do? He went forth into the kingdom, stopping at every house and castle, inquiring of every woman he met "What is it that women most

desire?" Well, what a lot of different answers he got! Among them were:

"Women want to be beautiful, and to have fine things."

"Women want to be waited on."

"Women want to be free to do as they please with their lives."

"Women want to be trusted and to have high positions in life."

Every woman the knight spoke to seemed to have a different desire. The knight quite despaired of finding an answer that all women could agree to. So, as the allotted year neared its close, the knight turned homeward as he had promised the queen, even knowing that he would be executed for failing to find an answer.

As the knight traveled back through a dark and gloomy wood, he stumbled upon a very old woman sitting on the grass. She was hideous beyond imagining, but she spoke to the knight in a kindly way. "What is it you seek, young man?" she asked.

"Good mother," said the knight, "I am a dead man unless I can tell what thing it is that women most desire. If you could tell me that, I would give you anything you asked for!"

"Well then, is that a promise?" asked the loathly lady. "You will do the thing I ask of you in return?"

"I swear it by my honor!" said the knight.

The loathly lady then whispered in the knight's ear, and he nodded solemnly. "Be cheerful now!" said the loathly lady. "The response I've whispered will win you your life!"

Together they traveled back to the court, where the queen and her attendants waited for him. "Well, sir, what is the answer you've found during your lengthy quest?" asked the queen.

"My Queen," said the knight, "you may kill me if you see fit. But the answer I have discerned through my travels is that what women desire most is to have sovereignty over their households and their husbands."

The queen and her ladies whispered in excitement over this reply and decided that in the long run it was the right answer. "Your life is spared," said the queen. Then, as she and her attendants prepared to leave the courtroom, the loathly lady stopped them with

her announcement: "This knight has promised to grant the first favor I ask of him, in return for my supplying the right answer," she said. "And the favor I ask is that he marry me."

"Oh, no," the knight wailed. "Take my money! Take my land! But do not ask that I wed you! What an awful fate for me and for my family, to marry someone old and ugly and poor!"

But the queen and her ladies agreed with the loathly lady: A promise is a promise.

Most weddings are accompanied by joy and celebration, but you can take my word for it that *this* wedding was a dismal affair. The knight married the old hag at daybreak in a very private ceremony and promptly hid her behind a curtain in his house. "My heart is breaking!" he said to her.

"What is the cause of your despair?" said the loathly lady from her curtained room. "I think your attitude is silly! What is it that men of your rank want? Surely you are not the best of humanity. You carry off young women who do not want you. You think your wealth sets you above all others. You scorn those who are poor and of lowly birth. You are interested only in pleasure and conquest. I ask you now to tell me truly: which is better to have, a loathly wife who can wisely advise, direct, and rule you, or a young and beautiful wife who has no wisdom and is apt to go flying off carelessly on her whims? I'll tell you this: I can be whichever one you prefer!"

The knight considered all that the muffled voice behind the curtain said to him and thought about the

lessons he had learned. After a while he said, "I must admit that I have put myself entirely in your power and have relied upon and been saved by your wisdom. So I promise that I will love you and be faithful to you. Whatever you desire shall also please me."

"You have answered well," said the woman. "Lift up the curtain and kiss me. You shall find that you can have both loveliness and wisdom, all in one person."

The knight lifted the curtain as directed and saw a maiden fairer than he could ever have imagined. They embraced one another and ever after obeyed one another in all the ways that add to mutual happiness.

"So you see," said the Wife of Bath, "that fate should bring all of us husbands who are young and strong. And may bad fortune attend all men who are not governed by their wives!" ◆

The Pardoner's Tale

**rologue:** Our Host next turned to the Pardoner, who was certainly an ugly fellow, with waxy hair and glaring eyes, and a voice like the bleating of a goat. "What do you say, Pardoner?" said the Host. "You seem to like to talk a great deal. Can you use that voice to tell us a tale with a moral?"

"When I preach in church," said the Pardoner, "I always use the same moral: *Money is the root of all evil.* Now, I myself love money better than anything else in the world, so I can be quite persuasive on the subject of it.

With my moral tales, I can stir simple people into opening their purses and giving me money for the worthless things I carry around with me. I call these things holy relics, but of course they're not. So, though I'm not a moral man, I can tell a moral tale with the best of them—which I will do now, if you'll be quiet."

The Three Thieves

Some time ago in Flanders there were three foolish, wicked men who spent their time cheating others and gambling in taverns. As they sat drinking and swearing one day at an inn, they heard the church bells toll for a funeral procession.

One of the men called to the serving boy and said, "What corpse is passing by this time?"

"It's an old companion of yours," said the boy. "Just last night, he was sitting here laughing and carousing. Then Death came and slew him suddenly. You know that Death has slain thousands around here during this plague. So I'd advise you to beware of him!"

"By my boots!" said one of the wicked men to the others. "Let us seek this fellow Death and kill

him. He who has taken so many others shall himself be dead by nightfall."

The three men swore a pact to act together as brothers in this task and went lurching out onto the highway to begin their search for Death. They had not gone far at all before they met a wretched-looking old man. The old man greeted them politely, saying "God protect you, my lords."

But the three companions sneered rudely at him, and one of them jeered, "You're a sorry sight, ancient one, all wrapped up in a cloak! How does someone so old as you stay alive?"

"Why?" said the old man. "Because I cannot find anyone who will exchange his youth for my old age. And because Death cannot take me, though I might walk from here to India. My bones will never be at rest. But I would advise you, lads, not to speak so rudely to old people. For one day, if you're lucky, you may be old, too. And now I must be on my way."

But one of the men stopped him roughly, "Wait a minute, you old rogue! Since you speak so

familiarly of Death, he must be a friend of yours, this Death who goes about killing us young folks! Tell us where he is, or we'll make you pay dearly."

"Why, if you want to find Death," said the old man, "I left him just near here in the woods under an oak tree."

The three wicked fellows said nothing more to the old man and went running off to the oak tree. There they found a great pile of gold coins, perhaps about eight bushels of them. Dazzled by the sight of such wealth, they simply gazed at it for a while, until the worst of the three said, "Listen, brothers, Fortune has given us this treasure so that we can live in ease and pleasure forever more. But we can't carry the coins back to town during daylight, for people will think we stole them. So we must wait here until nightfall and then carry the treasure home slyly and in secret. However, night's a long way off, and we'll need bread and wine to see us through the day. So let's draw straws. The one who gets the shortest straw shall go back to town to get our food and drink, while the other two of us stay here to guard the treasure."

So the three drew straws, and the lot fell to the youngest man, who—as agreed—started back to town. As soon as he had left, the man who had thought up this plan said to his companion, "I'll tell you something for your own good. There is a great deal of gold here. You and I would each come away with a larger share if we could divide it into halves instead of into thirds."

"How can that be done?" asked the other man. "Our young partner knows we have the gold."

" I have a plan," said the first villain. "When the lad comes back with the food, you get up and start wrestling with him as if in fun. And while you're pretending to play, I'll stab the fellow dead."

So the two agreed to kill their companion in this way when he returned. In the meantime, as the youngest villain walked to town, he thought, "Imagine if I could have all that gold to myself! Why, I'd never have another care in the world!" Then it came into his wicked head that if he poisoned his companions, he would have their shares of the treasure as well as his own.

Walking swiftly to town, the young man went to a druggist and said he needed poison for killing rats in a barn. This purchase made, the fellow went on to buy the bread and then to a shop to buy three bottles of wine. Into two of these he poured the poison.

When he returned to his comrades, they killed him as they had planned. That done, one of them said, "Now let us drink and be merry!" And so saying, he picked up one of the wine bottles, drank from it, and passed it to his companion.

So were all three villains slain. For they had found Death under the oak tree, as the old man had told them, though they did not recognize Death in a pile of gold. ◆

The Nun's Priest's Tale

Prologue: Many of the pilgrims' tales had been quite solemn and dreary, full of woe and suffering. "Can we not have a cheerful story?" asked the Host. "How about you, Priest? You seem to be sulking because your horse is so old and skinny. Why don't you cheer yourself and us up by telling a jolly tale?" Immediately the priest launched into this story:

Chanticleer and Pertelote

There was once a widow and her two daughters. They

100

were very poor and dined on bread and milk, not roast meat and wine as rich folks do. Bacon was a rare treat. And they shared their dwelling with a cow and three pig and a sheep named Moll. Things were not very tidy indoors. But outdoors was their prize possession: a cock whose name was Chanticleer.

Ah, what a fine rooster Chanticleer was! His comb was coral-red with jagged black edges, his bill was jet black, his legs and toes were azure blue, his nails were lily-white, and his feathers were gold. Every hen in the flock was in love with Chanticleer, but his ladylove was Pertelote, a wise and lovely bird upon whom he relied for her frankness and wisdom.

Now it happened one night that Chanticleer had a dreadful nightmare, and he woke Pertelote to tell her about it. "Oh, I am sick with this dream!" said Chanticleer. "In it, I was roaming about the yard, and a beast who was something between yellow and red grabbed me. The beast was much like a dog, but he had a thin snout and eyes that glowed. The very memory of him fills me with fear!"

"What a coward you are to be afraid of dreams!" said Pertelote. "Dreams are caused by indigestion. Everyone knows that. I will get you some herbs that will cure your stomach. All you need is to peck some castor beans, caper berries, or ivy leaves, and perhaps some nice worms to top it off. Cheer up, husband! And don't be afraid of dreams. They mean nothing."

"I rely on your wisdom as a rule, my dear," responded Chanticleer. "But I can't help thinking that you are wrong about dreams. Why, I remember the old story of the two travelers. You know the tale: There was no cottage that could house them both one night, so they stayed in different places. The first traveler had a dream in which his companion cried 'Help me, dear friend, I am dying of my wounds!' The dreamer turned over restlessly and went back to sleep. But in the morning he saw a cart that bore the body of his dead friend, who as it turned out had been murdered for his money."

"That story is nonsense!" said Pertelote. "I can't believe that you're trembling over other people's

eyes watched him hungrily. These were the eyes of Reynard the Fox, ever eager for a tidbit of chicken meat from the farmyard.

Nearby in the cabbage patch, the two met—Reynard and Chanticleer. The handsome rooster had never seen a fox before, and alarmed by Reynard's shiny eyes, turned away.

"Ah, please don't leave!" protested Reynard. "How cheerful your song makes me! Truly, it reminds me of your dear father! His was a voice as splendid as yours. I rejoiced in listening to that incredible rooster. His music was a gift to the ears of all who were privileged to hear it."

"Indeed?" said Chanticleer, stopping in his tracks. He was happy to hear these words of praise for his lineage.

"He was different from you, though, in one important way," Reynard continued. "When your father sang, he would close his eyes and stretch out his neck. In this way, the sounds of the music came out clearer and purer."

"Oh, I can do that, too!" said Chanticleer. Shutting his eyes and

dreams as well as your own! Where is the brave and sensible rooster you once were?"

"Nonsense the story may be," said Chanticleer. "But so are the herbal remedies you recommend. Nevertheless, I will try to adopt your attitude about dreams, my love. I shall approach this day with the courage you admire in me."

With these words, Chanticleer strutted out into the yard, full of happiness at the spring weather and confident in the advice of his lovely wife. How merrily he sang, crowing love songs about his beloved Pertelote, even while two glowing

arching his neck as gracefully as he imagined his father had done, he let out the first words of his love song about Pertelote. And of course it was at this moment, while the vain rooster's eyes were closed, that Reynard grabbed him by the throat and set off with him to the fox den, there to make a meal of him.

The hens in the yard saw this encounter and attack and set up a cackling and cry that brought the widow and her daughters to the door. These women, seeing their prize rooster carried off, called their neighbors for help. Then there began such a hooting and racket as you've never heard, with people yelling and chasing after Reynard. It was as if the sky would fall down with their hollering.

Caught though he was in Reynard's jaws, Chanticleer could still speak. "Is this not insulting to you, that all these people think they can catch you?" coughed Chanticleer. "Why do you not tell them they are fools and command them to go away?"

"You are right, and I'll do it at once," said Reynard. But of course, the moment he opened his mouth to say these words, Chanticleer escaped and flew to the highest branch of the tallest tree.

"Have I offended you in some way?" said the frustrated Reynard. "Do come down, friend. I never meant you any harm."

" Oh, no!" said Chanticleer. "I'll not fall for your flattery again! There is no excuse for people who close their eyes when they most need to see."

"Well," grumbled Reynard, "neither is there excuse for those who jabber when they should keep silent."

The Priest brought his story to an end by saying. "This is not just a silly tale about a rooster, dreams, bad advice, and a fox. There are many lessons in this story, and it's up to you find the morals in it." ♦

Medieval Glossary

epic a narrative poem that celebrates the feats of a real or legendary hero

fable a story about legendary persons that often makes a moral point

fabliau a medieval verse tale characterized by comic treatment of themes drawn from real life

fairy tale a fanciful tale of legendary deeds and creatures, usually intended for children

fantasy a story that is fanciful and may contain supernatural events

feudalism a political and economic system of Europe in the Middle Ages, centered on a landholding lord and his relations to vassals

fief the estate of a feudal lord

knight a medieval gentleman-soldier, usually a vassal

legend a popular, sometimes fictional story handed down through history

liege lord a lord to whom a knight or vassal owes allegiance

lord a man of high rank in feudal society, such as a king or owner of a manor

manor an area of land controlled by a lord during medieval times

minstrel a medieval entertainer who traveled from place to place to sing songs and recite poetry

myth a traditional story with supernatural creatures and heros that serves to explain the world view of a people

serf a member of the serving class in medieval Europe, bound to the land and owned by a lord

troubadour a poet in medieval times who composed poems and songs for kings and other nobles

vassal a person who held land from a feudal lord and received protection in exchange for allegiance to that lord.

yeoman a farmer who farmed his own small plot of land in medieval England

TEACHER'S ANNOTATED
Bibliography

Fortunately, the Middle Ages are not only fascinating to young people, but to adults, too. Here's an annotated bibliography for *you*. Most of the titles have been selected because they are great reads as well as accurate and thorough presentations of medieval life. Some of the books (e.g., 1 below) are visual delights that you may want to share with your students.

1. **Bain, Iain.** *Celtic Key Patterns* (Sterling 1994). This is a guide to the knotwork, spirals, and interlaced figures used by the medieval Celts in ornaments and manuscripts. Color plates show the intricacy of the designs, and diagrams then show how to reconstruct them. The geometry of it all will intrigue students and encourage them to use math and measurement skills to make their own designs, especially as they create their illuminated day books (page 40). A fine companion book is Eva Wilson's *Early Medieval Designs from Britain* (Dover 1983).

2. **Bishop, Morris.** *The Middle Ages* (American Heritage Press 1970) If you like to read history organized around major concepts and themes, Bishop's book will appeal to you. The chapters "The Life of Thought" and "The Artist's Legacy" are particularly useful.

3. **Collis, Louise.** *Memoirs of a Medieval Woman: The Life and Times Of Margery Kempe.* (Harper Colophon 1983). This is the biography of a woman who journeyed across Europe from England to the Holy Land, leaving her fourteen children behind as she went on a pilgrimage. Kempe met mendicants and dignitaries, got into some hair-raising scrapes, and survived a dreadful journey in the hold of a Venetian boat. The book reads like a novel. You might have fun comparing Margery Kempe to Chaucer's independent and fiesty Wife of Bath. (See page 91.)

4. **Fife, Graeme.** *Arthur the King.* (Sterling 1991). For adult readers, Fife concentrates on how stories about Arthur developed, beginning in the Celtic heartland, living on and traveling through the courts of Europe, and staying with us even today in books, movies, and plays. The book is a concentrated, detailed study appealing to all of us who are still fascinated by the Once and Future King.

5. **Gies, Frances, and Joseph Gies.** *Cathedral, Forge, and Water Wheel* (HarperCollins 1994). When lucidly set as here in its human context, technology can be fascinating. The Gies show how innovative medieval Europeans were in developing tools and techniques for farms, industry, navigation, and war, and how much of the technology originated in China, India, and the Middle East.

6. Gies, Frances, and Joseph Gies. *Marriage and the Family in the Middle Ages* (1989); *Life in a Medieval Castle* (1974); *Life in a Medieval Village* (1990) (all Harper paper). The Gies are scholars who have mined the social history of the Middle Ages and write about it with clarity and much human interest and appeal. You might share these books with some of your better readers as they do follow-up research. Also see the Gies's *Women in the Middle Ages* (1987) and *Life in a Medieval City* (1969) (paper, Harper Perennial Library).

7. Guerber, H. A. *Myths and Legends of the Middle Ages* (Dover 1993). This is a reprint of a book originally published in 1909, and after you dip into it you can see why it has been reissued and has gained new fans. There are stories, faithfully retold, of Beowulf, Charlemagne, Titurel and the Holy Grail, Tristan and Iseult, El Cid, and many more. The stories are long and sometimes complicated, but the book can be a great resource for you if you're looking for medieval tales that you can peruse first and then tell aloud in your own way.

8. *The Oxford History of Medieval Europe*, edited by George Holmes. (paper, Oxford University Press 1988). This is a definitive history of the entire thousand-year-long period. While you may not have time to plow through the whole thing, you'll find it a fine source of answers to questions your students may raise as they explore the Middle Ages. The index is clear and complete, and there is a useful Chronology chart.

9. Tuchman, Barbara W. *A Distant Mirror: The Calamitous 14th Century*. (paper, Ballantine Books 1979). Tuchman writes so felicitously and throws such new light on her subject that this book was on the best-seller list for more than nine months. *A Distant Mirror* shows two contradictory images of the declining years of the Middle Ages: a time of chivalry, cathedrals, crusades, and breathtaking art; and a time of spiritual despair and political chaos.

10. Wilson, Elizabeth B. *Bibles and Bestiaries: A Guide to Illuminated Manuscripts* (Farrar, Straus and Giroux 1994) You'll want to share this one with your students. While there have been many books on illuminated manuscripts, few have been designed for young readers or illustrated so beautifully. The art comes from the collection of the Pierpont Morgan Library. The text begins with handmade books and concludes with the invention of printing. Included is a chapter on best-sellers of the Middle Ages.

STUDENT'S ANNOTATED
Bibliography

In these listings, numerals in parentheses give the approximate grade level of the book. Any numeral in boldface at the end of an annotation suggests to which anthology story the book is particularly suited as follow-up reading. For example, **1** refers to *Beowulf*, the first story in this anthology. In general, however, the books can be used across the board for enjoyment and for enrichment as your students pursue the aspects of the Middle Ages that interest them most.

HISTORY

1. **Adams, Simon.** *The Middle Ages: AD 456 to 1450.* (Warwick 1990) (4–8) Students can find out here what was happening in other parts of the world during Europe's Middle Ages.

2. **Adams, Brian.** *Medieval Castles.* (Watts 1989) (3–5) You might use this in conjunction with the poster as students study the interior features of different kinds of castles.

3. **Adkins, Jan.** *The Art and Industry of Sandcastles.* (Walker 1994) (3–6) This is a wonderfully quirky book that utilizes the experience of building sandcastles to launch a pictorial study of castle construction through the ages, beginning with primitive Saxon forts. An inspiration for model builders! **1**

4. **Aliki.** *A Medieval Feast.* (HarperCollins 1983) (2–6) The king and his court are coming to visit a lord and his lady, and the castle staff, from hunters and hawkers to cooks and servers, readies the feast. Aliki's wonderful illustrations are based on late medieval manuscripts. **3**

5. **Biesty, Stephen.** *Stephen Biesty's Cross-Sections Castle.* (Dorling Kindersley 1994). (3–6) Big, detailed drawings stress the castle's primary function as a fortress to ward off an attack and also as a community where many kinds of workers labored during times of peace. **1**

6. **Byam, Michael.** *Arms and Armor.* (Knopf 1988) (4–7) A volume in the Eyewitness Books series, Byam's history covers weaponry from the Stone Age to modern times. There are several sections that deal with arms and armor of the Middle Ages. Illustrations and their captions are extremely detailed. Many boys will be enthralled with this book.

Suggest that they imagine what it was like to wear all that armor! **1, 2, 3**

7. Caselli, Giovanni. *The Everyday Life of a Cathedral Builder.* (Peter Bedrik 1987) (4–7) Readers learn about the building of a cathedral from the point of view of a young apprentice architect. The fine illustrations include details about Rheims and Chartres cathedrals. **2, 7**

8. Caselli, Giovanni. *The Middle Ages* (Peter Bedrik 1988) (4–7) Here are some memorable descriptions ranging over many aspects of medieval life: craft fairs, markets, the life of farmers, entertainment, along with knights and crusades. **4, 5, 6, 7**

9. Corbishley, Mike. *Medieval World* (Hamlyn 1993) (4–8) This book provides a great way to launch into a multicultural study of the sixth-through-fifteenth centuries. Through timelines, illustrations, and text, Corbishley shows what was happening in Western Europe, Africa, India, Asia, and the Americas during that period.

10. *Fourteenth Century Towns,* edited by John D. Clare. (Harcourt 1993) (4–8) Like others in the Living History series, the illustrations in this volume are photos of models wearing clothes of the period and reenacting situations and events. While this strategy may not be to every reader's taste, the book does provide a wealth of facts about how religion, guilds, schools, the Black Death, and constant warfare affected the lives of ordinary people. There's also a timeline and a map of Europe in 1360. **4, 5, 6, 7**

11. Gravett, Christopher. *Castle* (Dorling Kindersley 1994) (4–7) Wonderful photos and concise legends and captions show many aspects of castle life, from the animals that actually lived in the castle to the serfs who worked outside to provide food for the nobles. The genesis of castles is made clear, and there's an interesting side trip to a Japanese castle. **1, 2, 3**

12. Howarth, Sarah. *Medieval People* (Millbrook 1992) (4–6) The class system during the Middle Ages was complex, but Howarth does a good job of explaining it, using photographs of paintings, sculptures, illuminated manuscripts, and stained glass windows to illustrate her points. **4, 5, 6, 7**

13. Hunt, Jonathan. *Illuminations* (Macmillan 1993) (3–6) This is a sophisticated, nicely illustrated alphabet book (from *alchemist* to *zither*) with illuminated capitals that may inspire your students to make similar books of their own. Much of the text refers to King Arthur and the Arthurian legends. **2, 3**

14. *Knights in Armor,* edited by John D. Clare (Harcourt 1992) (4–8) This Living History volume (see 10, above) is valuable in its vivid descriptions of how a young man earned knighthood and of the tasks that awaited him thereafter as a professional soldier. The book concludes with a section called *How Do We Know?*, a summary of how historians work and the materials they use. **2, 3**

15. Macaulay, David. *Castle* (Houghton 1977) (3–8) Long before "Where's Waldo?" appeared on the scene, Macaulay understood the avid interest young readers have in exploring visual details. This interest is directed toward understanding how a medieval castle was built. There's also a glossary of terms associated with construction. You may want to use this book to supplement the poster. **1, 3**

16. Macaulay, David. *Cathedral: The Story of Its Construction* (Houghton 1973) (3–8) From architect's plans to craftspeople's labor, medieval cathedrals took many decades to reach completion. Here Macaulay focuses on the labor and details involved in the construction of a French Gothic cathedral. **2, 7**

17. Macdonald, Fiona. *A Medieval Cathedral* (Peter Bedrik 1991) (3–6) The illustrations (by John James) are detailed cutaways. The text tells not only how a cathedral was built, but also about the day-to-day life of the people around it. **2, 4, 6, 7**

18. Ruby, Jennifer. *Costumes in Context: Medieval Times* (Batsford 1990) (5–7) What did people wear back then? Ruby shows us, through drawings and descriptions. If your class is planning plays based on medieval events, or writing and illustrating stories about that era, this book is a fine source of ideas **3, 4, 5, 6, 7**

19. Sancha, Sheila. *Walter Dragun's Town: Crafts and Trades in the Middle Ages* (HarperCollins 1989) (4–8) Through covering just one week's events in Stamford, England, during the Middle Ages, Sancha manages to introduce the interactions between merchants and craftspeople. The drawings bring the people and their activities to life. **4, 5, 6, 7**

20. Suskind, Richard. *Men in Armor: The Story of Knights and Knighthood* (Norton 1968) What makes this book especially worthwhile is the way it weaves history into the story of how one young man seeks to become a knight. **2, 3**

FICTION

1. Anderson, Margaret J. *In the Keep of Time* (Knopf 1977) (5–8) Four children time trip back to medieval Scotland, via a door in Smailholm Tower, an ancient border keep.

2. Chaucer, Geoffrey. *Canterbury Tales* Translated and adapted by Barbara Cohen (Lothrop 1988) (4–8) Four of the Chaucer tales are here beautifully illustrated by Trina Schart Hyman. **7**

3. Corrin, Sara, and Stephen Corrin. *The Pied Piper of Hamelin* (Harcourt 1989). (3–6) This legend is based on a real incident in Germany in 1284. The illustrative paintings by Errol Le Cain are somberly Brueghel-like. **5, 6**

4. Cushman, Karen. *Catherine, Called Birdy* (Clarion 1994) (6–8) Catherine is an outspoken 13-year-old who lives in a medieval English village. She has much to say about her day-to-day life there, especially about her father's plans to arrange a marriage for her. **3**

5. de Angeli, Marguerite. *The Door in the Wall* (Doubleday 1949; Dell paper)(3–6) A physically disabled boy trains as a page as he seeks knighthood, then deals with an unexpected circumstance that changes his goals. The book won a Newbery award in 1950. **1, 2**

6. Dickinson, Peter. *Merlin Dreams* (Delacorte 1988) (5–7) And his dreams are nine wonderful tales of the Middle Ages! **2**

7. Gray, Elizabeth J., *Adam of the Road* (Viking 1942; Puffin paper) (4–7) Adam travels the highways of medieval England, searching for his minstrel father and his kidnapped dog. The book was the Newbery winner in 1943. **4, 5, 6**

8. Hastings, Selina. *Reynard the Fox* (Tambourine 1990) (3–5) The roguish, deceitful Reynard is the hero of many medieval tales (see *Chanticleer and Pertelote* on page 100 in this volume.) Hastings shows him at his most outrageous pranks as he contends with judge and jury. **6, 10**

9. Hastings, Selina. *Sir Gawain and the Loathly Lady* (Lothrop 1985) (3–6) Here's another tale that Chaucer borrowed and gave to the Wife of Bath to tell in her own way. In Hastings' version, it's King Arthur who must answer the riddle and then promise one of his knights to the lady. **2, 7**

10. Hodges, Margaret. *Saint George and the Dragon* (Little, Brown 1984) (3–6) At the request of the princess Una, the Red Cross Knight sets out to kill the beast that plagues her kingdom. This is a felicitous retelling of Edmund Spenser's 16th-century epic "The Faerie Queen." **2, 7**

11. Jacques, Brian. *Redwall* (Philomel 1987) (5–7) A rat named Cluny the Scourge threatens Redwall Abbey, and Matthias the mouse sets out to save it. This is far more than an "animal tale," for it brilliantly and accurately presents medieval lifestyles. **2, 7**

12. Lasker, Joe. *A Tournament of Knights* (Harper 1986) (3–6) Lord Justin prepares to fight in his first tournament. **2, 3**

13. Lewis, Naomi. *Proud Knight, Fair Lady: The Twelve Lais of Marie De France.* (Viking 1989) (5–7) Marie De France wrote allegories and moral tales. (*The Story of the Little Bird* on page 54 is often attributed to her.) The tales provide adept readers with insights into the society of the Middle Ages, and often into the psychology of women who were restricted to hearth and home. **3, 4**

14. Pierce, Tamora. *Alanna: The First Adventure Song of the Lioness* (Atheneum 1983) (5–7) The heroine changes places with her twin brother and becomes a knight. **2, 3**

15. Skurzynski, Gloria. *The Minstrel in the Tower* (Random 1988) (3–4) After their father is killed in the Crusades, a brother and sister search for their uncle. **4**

16. Skurzynski, Gloria. *What Happened in Hamelin* (Four Winds 1979) (5–6) The harrowing story is told by Geist, a baker's apprentice, who stayed behind after the Pied Piper led the other children away. (Also see the Corrins' book, above.) **5, 6**

17. **Stearns, Pamela.** *Into the Painted Bear's Lair* (Houghton 1976) (4–6) Gregory enlists the help of Sir Rosemary, a female knight, to get him out of a bear's den.

18. **Sutcliff, Rosemary.** *Beowulf* (Peter Smith 1984) (5–7) Sutcliff retells the story of Beowulf's battle with Grendel. **1**

19. **Sutcliff, Rosemary.** *Tristan and Iseult* (Dutton 1971) (5–7) The story of these star-crossed lovers of medieval days is also the source of Richard Wagner's opera *Tristan und Isolde.* Sutcliff has also written other books on medieval themes: *The Light Beyond the Forest, The Sword and the Circle,* and *The Road to Camlan* (all Dutton).

20. **Temple, Frances.** *The Ramsay Scallop* (Orchard 1994) (5–7) Elenor and her bethrothed, Thomas, are reluctant to wed. They make a pilgrimage to Spain and are brought together as friends through their numerous adventures. **7**

BIOGRAPHY

1. **Brooks, Polly Schoyer.** *Beyond the Myth: The Story of Joan of Arc* (HarperCollins 1990)

2. **Brooks, Polly Schoyer.** *Queen Eleanor: Independent Spirit of the Medieval World.* (HarperCollins 1983)

3. **Dramer, Kim.** *Kublai Khan* (Chelsea 1990)

4. **Fritz, Jean.** *The Man Who Loved Books* (Putnam 1981) A biography of Saint Columba

5. **Humble, Richard.** *The Travels of Marco Polo* (Watts 1990)

6. **Jessop, Joanne.** *Richard the Lionhearted* (Watts 1989)

7. **McCaughrean, Geraldine.** *El Cid* (Oxford 1989) Epic of the Spanish hero

8. **Rockwell, Anne.** The *Boy Who Drew Sheep* (Athenaeum 1973). A biography of Giotto de Bandanna, the famous Italian painter

9. **Simian, Charnan** *Leif Eriksson and the Vikings: The Norse Discovery of America* (Children's Press 1991)

RECORDINGS

1. Music There's been a general upsurge of interest in medieval music, mostly because of our rediscovery of the exquisite harmonies of the voices. The following are among the best of the CDs. Each comes with an extensive brochure that tells about the music's place in medieval life.

♦ ***Chant*** (Angel Records) is a collection of Gregorian chants sung by the monks of Santo Domingo de Silos in Spain. This monastery was a way station for medieval pilgrims, and this is the music they listened to as they rested for a while during their journey.

♦ ***Hildegard Von Bingen: Symphoniae*** (Deutsche Harmonia Mondi). Hildegarde (born 1098) was a mystic who was couragous enough (in a man's world) to compose and write down her own liturgical music and poetry. For its time—and even for ours—her music is quite original and often strange.

♦ ***On Yoolis Night: Medieval Carols and Motets*** (Harmonia Mundi France) These lovely songs are presented by the Anonymous 4, a group of women who specialize in the discovery and performance of medieval music.

♦ ***The Unicorn*** (Erato) Anne Azema takes listeners on a musical journey through medieval France. Included are songs about nature, about imaginary beasts, and about spinning and weaving.

2. Stories For a wonderful storyteller's versions of Arthurian tales, try Jim Weiss's *King Arthur and His Knights*, an hour-long tape recording (Greathall Productions). The recording has won awards from the American Library Association and the Parent's Choice Foundation. Among the stories are *The Sword in the Stone*, *The Round Table*, *Two Rude Knights*, and *Guinevere*.

3. Videos As you know, videos are expensive to purchase. Your library may help you borrow the following:

♦ ***The Crusades: October 2, 1187*** (30 minutes) (6–8) Zenger Video

♦ ***David Macaulay's Castle*** (58 minutes) (3–8) PBS Video

♦ ***Illuminated Lives: A Brief History of Women's Work in the Middle Ages*** (6 minutes) (3–6) International Film Bureau

♦ ***Medieval Times: Life in the Middle Ages*** (30 minutes) (6–8) Howard Niles (With a guide and worksheets)